MAUI
REMEMBERS
A LOCAL HISTORY

NOTES ON THE HAWAIIAN LANGUAGE

Recognizing the responsibility we all share for the correct pronunciation of Hawaiian words, *Maui Remembers* has supplied the necessary diacritics. The two diacritical marks used in Hawaiian are the macron (ˉ) and the glottal stop ('). The macron, or kahakō in Hawaiian, indicates an elongated vowel sound. Vowels with no macron are to be pronounced:

a like a in above

e like e in bet

i like y in city

o like o in sole

u like oo in moon

The macron asks the speaker to stress the vowel by making it somewhat longer. The glottal stop, 'u'ina in Hawaiian, indicates the sound between the ohs in the English oh-oh.

Now with this in mind, try Hāli'imaile and Pu'unēnē!

Diacritical marks are used for Hawaiian words and place names in *Maui Remembers*, but could not always be ascertained for personal names. *The Hawaiian Dictionary*, 1986, *Place Names of Hawai'i*, 1974, and the University of Hawai'i *Map of Maui*, 1988, were used as the primary sources for correct spelling.

MAUI
REMEMBERS
A LOCAL HISTORY

TEXT BY GAIL BARTHOLOMEW
PHOTO RESEARCH BY BREN BAILEY

**MUTUAL
PUBLISHING**

Design
Michael Horton Design

First Printing August 1994
1 2 3 4 5 6 7 8 9

ISBN 1-56647-069-2   Case
ISBN 1-56647-070-6   Soft

Mutual Publishing
1127 11th Avenue, Mezz. B
Honolulu, Hawaii 96816
Telephone (808) 732-1709
Fax (808) 734-4094

Printed in Taiwan

PREFACE

This book is long overdue! At last, Maui's extraordinary history is available to all. *Maui Remembers: A Local History* dramatically documents Maui's unique con-tributions to Hawaiian history.

We have often been asked how long it took to compile this book. From the time we put ideas into action, three years have transpired. But it was more than 20 years ago when we first became fascinated with Maui history and began compiling information and photos for some unknown future use. As a consequence, we could not possibly properly acknowledge the many researchers, authors and Maui residents who have assisted during that time. The acknowledgments that follow represent the tip of the iceberg, or shall we say the tip of Haleakalā?

Several persons reviewed sections of *Maui Remembers* for historical accuracy. Thanks go to Donne Dawson of Alexander & Baldwin, Jim Luckey and Barbara Sharp of the Lahaina Restoration Foundation, Hōkūlani Holt-Padilla of Nā Pua Noʻeau, Dawn Duensing, Nolemanu Hu, Mark Scruggs, and Dana Nāone Hall. Jay Van Zwalenburg gave her attention to the entire manuscript.

For assistance with the location and identification of photos, we are particularly indebted to Sylvia Hunt of Maui Land and Pineapple Company, Jeff White of the Hawaiʻi State Archives, Camille Lyon of Haleakalā Ranch, and Casey Dunnill, who gave us so much of their time and energy. Their enthusiasm matched ours. DeSoto Brown

gave us the gift of guidance, a priceless commodity. These treasures deserve a mahalo nui loa.

The book's photo collection was enhanced greatly through the efforts of Dawn Duensing, Nina Sachdeva and the staff at the Bishop Museum Visual Collections, the Maui Historical Society Museum staff (especially Kealiʻi Reichel), Ruth Baldwin and family, Carol and Randy von Tempsky, Kahului Trucking & Storage, Kwan Hi Lim, Boogie Wainui, Na Kai ʻEwalu, Dana Nāone Hall, Barbara Sharp and the Lahaina Restoration Foundation, Sonny Gamponia, Henry E. Meyer, Jr. and Irving Jenkins. We are grateful for Alexander & Baldwin's help through Gaylord Kubota of the A&B Sugar Museum, and Yvette Ho. Thanks to each and every person willing to share their precious photos!

Several librarians and archivists lent their expertise to the text of the book, including Jeff White of the Hawaiʻi State Archives, Ann Marsteller of the Hawaiian Sugar Planters Association Library, Marilyn Reppun of the Hawaiian Mission Children's Society Library, and Chieko Tachihata of the Hawaiian Collection at the University of Hawaiʻi. Thanks go to Lani Scott and Maurice Zane at the Kahului Public Library who made the wealth of their Hawaiian collection available. Carla Mauri of the Makawao Public Library generously gave of her time. Thanks also to Dorothy Tolliver, Lillian Mangum and Alice Ono of the Maui Community College Library who provided support and assistance.

Several people helped to clarify

perplexing questions, including Bob and Donald Hughes, Ruth Kihm Molina, Bill Tavares, Peter Baldwin, Carol Wilcox, Edna Taufaasau, Elaine Wender, Hal Wright, and Sue Nakashima. Hōkūlani Holt-Padilla gave invaluable guidance in the use of the Hawaiian language.

For assorted assistance, we want to thank Ric Martini, Victor Pellegrino, Kelly Arbor, Beverly Young, Jamie Woodburn, Naomi Tanizaki, Roan Browne and David Rick. Kris Shibano and Pat Richards provided computer support. Ed Bartholomew put in many hours as editor-in-chief. Ivy Bartholomew acted admirably as a research assistant, and Kate Bartholomew helped with clerical chores. Thanks to Lisa Spence of Roy's Photo Center and Nancy Edgerly of Bay Photo for technical assistance, and to Zach and Luke Bailey for retrieving and delivering innumerable photos.

Taking on this challenging task and, more importantly, completing it, could not have been done without the encouragement of the late Tommy Holmes to it get started, and our husbands, Fred Bailey and Ed Bartholomew, for support throughout the entire process.

While we have made every effort to provide accurate information from a wide variety of sources to provide a reliable Maui historical resource, there still may be errors. Those noting inaccuracies are encouraged to contact us.

Last of all, we want to thank Maui and its people. We are grateful for being able to live here and to share in its bounty and its warmth.

TABLE OF CONTENTS

MĀUI THE DEMIGOD

The Hawaiian island of Maui is blessed with a remarkable name, famed throughout the Pacific. It is named after Māui, the demigod, a figure almost without equal in the folklore of Polynesia. Māui's epic tales evolved as they travelled through vast time and distance, so accounts vary between island groups and even within islands. So it is that East Maui stories diverge from those of West Maui.

Although different in detail, Māui's adventures follow a common pattern. Māui was born of the goddess Hina. He earned his reputation as a rollicking trickster through his superhuman strength, daring and cunning, aided by his ability to appear and disappear at will. But Māui did far more than play tricks. Using his extraordinary strength and a magic fishhook, he singlehandedly dragged the islands of Hawai'i from the bottom of the sea - no mean feat! Among many other dazzling deeds, he discovered the secret of fire and elevated the sky to its present position.

His most memorable exploit, however, involved snaring the sun. Māui was living with his mother at Ka'uiki in Hāna when the sun took advantage of Māui's opening of the sky to arise from the lower world. Unfortunately, rather than arching the heavens at a leisurely pace which would allow people time to accomplish their daily tasks, the sun thoughtlessly chose to race across the sky. As Māui observed his mother's futile attempts to dry strips of kapa, or tapa, he resolved to check the sun's pace.

Determined to capture the sun in order to weaken its legs, Māui travelled to Kahakuloa to calculate its daily path. After viewing the sun's rise at the eastern end of Haleakalā, Māui returned home to announce his plan. Hina gave him many strong ropes and sent him to his grandmother, Mahuie, as this wise woman lived in the crater of Haleakalā, the house used by the sun.

Mahuie gave Māui one additional strong cord and, more importantly, good advice. He followed her directions and laid by a large wiliwili tree, awaiting his prey. The first ray, or leg, of the sun climbed the mountain straight into Māui's strong hands and secure rope. Māui grasped and tied each succeeding ray until the sun's 16 legs were fastened to the stalwart wiliwili tree, allowing him to attack the wayward sun with an adze. The terrified sun capitulated. A resulting pact with Māui forced the sun to dawdle for six months, yet allowed a faster pace for the remainder of the year. Once again, Māui, the clever one, had triumphed!

Māui at Haleakalā, House of the Sun. The island of Maui is named after this courageous and clever demigod.

ANCIENT MAUI - THE MODEL KINGDOM

Maui nō ka ʻoi! No question, Maui is the best and has been so for centuries. This age-old boast finds its roots in ancient Hawaiʻi, for, although Maui was not the largest, the most productive or populated, the other islands acknowledged Mauiʻs superiority. The reasons lie not only in its unsurpassed beauty, but also in chiefly wisdom and courage, wide political domain, and a fluke of geography.

Most beauty queens require time to primp and preen, and Maui was no exception. The islandʻs diverse splendor required a million years of preparation. Sisters, but not twins, the West Maui and Haleakalā volcanoes arose from the sea, then joined, first with each other and then with Molokaʻi, Lānaʻi and Kahoʻolawe, to form what is termed Maui Nui, or Great Maui. The rising sea level eventually separated these land masses, leaving the islands in their current configuration. Ever so slowly and relentlessly, rainfall, wind, and waves carved a varied landscape, while volcanism applied its rapid wrath to a swifter shaping. Pele, the volcano goddess, last added to the island in 1790, when Haleakalā exuded a fiery mass down its southern slope.

How was Maui populated? Archaeology tells us that the initial settlers arrived on successive voyages from the South Pacific, Polynesians possibly fleeing after defeat in war around 750 A.D. Once these early explorers discovered stands of endemic koa trees suitable for voyaging canoes, small groups braved a long and treacherous return to gather necessities and more settlers, for these colonizers had not found agricultural richness on Maui. Instead, they had encountered jungled valleys thick with hau, and needed to import what we now consider Hawaiian staples - taro, breadfruit, sweet potato, banana, coconut, pigs, dogs, chickens, ti, and wauke for making cloth.

The Hawaiian society that evolved was both sophisticated and successful. Food flourished in valleys, as well as on mountainous slopes, with the use of efficient irrigation dams, canals, terraces and erosion prevention methods. Excellent fishermen, innovative aquaculturists, and expert navigators, Hawaiians also exhibited skill in the crafting of kapa, canoes, carvings, mats and rock structures.

Hawaiian tradition taught that people and their ʻāina, or land, were one - thus spiritual parents Papa, the earth, and Wākea, the sky, gave birth to the island of Maui, as well as the high chiefs who ruled it. A complex feudal social system overseen by chiefs differing in degrees of divinity and authority competed for power through marriage, war and diplomacy.

Maui was divided into several chiefdoms prior to the sixteenth century. Domains periodically shifted, sometimes stretching beyond Mauiʻs shores. West Maui chief Kakaʻalaneo, along with his brother Kakaʻe, also ruled over Lānaʻi from a court in Lahaina. One of the most admired early chiefs, Kakaʻalaneo was known for his thrift, energy, and a reign free from strife and want.

In the 1500s, Kakaʻeʻs descendant, Piʻilani, pushed Maui to the fore politically as no one had done before. Piʻilaniʻs power extended from long-rebellious Hāna on one end of the island to the six West Maui bays, collectively called Honoapiʻilani, or bays acquired by Piʻilani, on the other end. The islands visible from Honoapiʻilani - Kahoʻolawe, Molokaʻi, and Lānaʻi - filled out Piʻilaniʻs vast dominion. This hands-on leader toured his expansive chiefdom, enforcing order and promoting industry. Piʻilaniʻs reign ushered in a long period of peace, stability, prosperity and a recognition of Maui as a model kingdom.

Famed for his energy and intelligence, Piʻilani constructed the West Maui phase of the noted Alaloa, or long road. His son Kihapiʻilani followed through by laying the East Maui section, completing the only ancient highway to encircle any Hawaiian island. Four to six feet wide and 138 miles long, this rock-paved thoroughfare, also known as the Kingʻs Highway, facilitated both peace and war, as it simplified travel and communication throughout the extended realm.

More often than not, Maui emerged triumphant in island wars. By usual standards, Maui should not have been so successful, as it ranked last of all the major islands in area cultivated, as well as number of communities. But Maui enjoyed the advantage of two highly concentrated population centers, one along the coast of West Maui and the other an area called Nā Wai ʻEhā, fed by the four streams of Waikapū, Waiheʻe, Waiehu and Wailuku. Maui's clever and courageous chiefs could easily access these resources in times of war.

A long-standing alliance with the island of Hawaiʻi fractured during the time a chief named Kekaulike reigned, but he was able to drive away subsequent invaders and maintain power. Kekaulike is best remembered, however, as the founder of the last Maui dynasty and, through three wives, as the father of a long line of influential Hawaiian royalty, including Kahekili, Boki, Keōpūolani, Queen Kaʻahumanu, King Kaumualiʻi of Kauaʻi, Regent Kīnaʻu, Princess Victoria Kamāmalu, the Kings Kamehameha II, III, IV and V, Queen Kapiʻolani, and Prince Kūhiō.

Although Kekaulike's son Kamehamehanui lost Hāna once again to the forces of the island of Hawaiʻi, his successor and brother Kahekili returned Hāna to the island fold. Not content with a unified island, Kahekili set out to force his model Maui kingdom on all the Hawaiian islands. No chief had ever ruled all of Hawaiʻi, but Kahekili was no ordinary chief.

Salt pans where sea water was extracted to obtain salt, Niu. Salt was used for drying fish and for flavoring.

Ancient Hawaiian bowl ornamented with teeth and bone.

3

Lahaina in the 18th Century.

A religious image, probably of Kamapuaʻa, a pig demigod, found in a Maui burial cave in 1963. The god of clouds and rain, Kamapuaʻa's domain stretched over the verdant windward coast.

Kalo, or taro, the most important food in ancient Hawaiʻi. Kalo's starchy root was used to make poi.

Hawaiian fisherman with throw net. Fish and shellfish constituted the major source of protein for Hawaiians.

KAMEHAMEHA AND KAHEKILI - CLASH OF WARRIORS

Kahekili was a warrior chief, ruthless and fierce. Reflecting his ferocious nature, as well as honoring the thunder god for which he was named, he tattooed one side of his body solid black. The most powerful Hawaiian ali'i, or chief, in the 1780s, Kahekili appeared the most likely winner of the race for conquest of the entire island group.

Kahekili, Maui's ali'i since 1736, held court at Wailuku. Though surrounded by several wives, it is said he fell in love with a young visitor named Keku'iapoiwa from the island of Hawai'i. When she returned home, she gave birth to a child who later echoed Kahekili's ambitions.

Without a doubt, Kahekili was ambitious. He usurped the island of O'ahu from his own adopted son, killing him in the process. He also tortured and killed most of the other O'ahu chiefs, building a macabre house with their skeletons. By 1786, Kahekili had a firm grip on Maui, O'ahu, Moloka'i and Lāna'i, and a compact with the chief of Kaua'i.

Kahekili's reign over this extended realm proved short-lived. An equally aggressive warrior named Kamehameha, the child Kahekili supposedly fathered, had been unable to dominate the island of Hawai'i despite ten years of war, so he turned eastward. In 1790,

Kamehameha proceeded to the island of Maui, his canoes heavy with firearms acquired from Westerners.

Kamehameha confronted the forces of Kahekili on the shores of the Ko'olau district at Hanawana. Successful in this first battle, he swiftly sailed his fleet of war canoes to Kahului, where more opposition awaited. Kamehameha's warriors forced the Maui men to retreat to steep-sided 'Iao Valley.

Kamehameha's firepower proved effective. Cannon balls aimed into 'Iao Valley slaughtered most of the Maui forces. So many were killed that their bodies dammed the blood-reddened Wailuku Stream. This battle of Kepaniwai, or water dam, gave Kamehameha hold over the entire island. But not for long.

Kamehameha's enemies on the Big Island had attacked his domain, necessitating his return. Taking advantage of Kamehameha's absence, Kahekili regained control of Maui. Not satisfied, Kahekili loaded his canoes with newly acquired guns and, backed by a fearsome-looking tattooed battalion with eyelids turned inside out, attacked Kamehameha in the waters surrounding the island of Hawai'i. With the assistance of foreign men, the warrior chiefs fought Hawai'i's first armed sea battle at Waipio to an indecisive conclusion.

Kahekili returned to O'ahu and died peacefully in 1794 at the age of 81, assigning the rule of Maui to

his half-brother Ka'eokūlani, who was subsequently killed along with his chiefs in a battle on O'ahu. In early 1795, Kamehameha, by then ruler of the entire island of Hawai'i and fortified once again by Western expertise and firearms, invaded and easily conquered Maui. Through a series of subsequent battles and agreements, Kamehameha attained his goal, reigning as the undisputed monarch of a united Hawaiian Islands.

On June 11 every year, Hawai'i celebrates the man who unified the islands. How easily fate could have transformed Kamehameha Day into Kahekili Day, an occasion to drape leis around a regal statue, half black from head to toe.

Kamehameha (1753-1819) as he looked when he first opposed Maui's powerful king Kahekili.

A young Kamehameha at spear practice. Kamehameha conquered Maui twice in his ultimately successful campaign to rule the Hawaiian Islands.

COOK AND LA PEROUSE - EUROPEAN DISCOVERERS

Captain James Cook, famed Pacific explorer, left his job undone. Although he was the first Westerner in Hawai'i, he missed the best island. It wasn't until his second trip that Cook even sighted Maui.

On November 26, 1779, Captain Cook sailed his ships *Discovery* and *Resolution* into view of Maui's northeast shore, but the rocky coast kept him from landing. The next day on his westward route, he approached Maui's central valley, the one for which Maui is nicknamed. Residents poured out in canoes and, according to Cook, "...came into the Ships without the least hesitation." Cook's most important visitor was Maui chief Kahekili. Self-assured and curious, Kahekili boarded the *Discovery*, showing his respect through the gift of a valued red feather cloak.

Following two days of barter for bananas, pigs and sweet potatoes, Cook departed eastward and, on November 30, anchored along the Hāna coast. The sight of the island of Hawai'i lured Cook further eastward, robbing him of the distinction of being the first Westerner on Maui's shores.

Seven years later, this honor went to Admiral Jean-Francois de Galaup, Comte de La Perouse, who spent all of three hours with feet firmly on the soil of Maui. The seasoned French explorer had departed Easter Island with his two frigates, the *Astrolabe* and the *Boussole*, seeking the exact position of the Hawaiian Islands, with particular interest in the unsurveyed island of Maui. He came into sight of the island on May 28, 1786, reaching a point some 20 miles offshore by nightfall. The next morning he skirted the Hāna coast, admiring the beauty of waterfalls, mountains, and verdant landscape, and observing numerous and populous native villages. Rough seas prevented the crew from going ashore and limited their trade with the 150 canoes of eager Hawaiians who attempted to barter.

Seeking a safe landing, La Perouse continued south, noting an ever-drier, more sparsely populated coast. Though far from satisfactory, he decided on Keone'ō'io as a site for further trading. And trade they did, with Hawaiians filling the ships with the squeals of 300 pigs within just a few hours. Captain de Langle of the *Astrolabe*, according to La Perouse, "had his decks in an instant crowded with a multitude of Indians. But they were so docile and so apprehensive of giving offence, that it was extremely easy to prevail on them to return to their boats. I had no idea of a people so mild and so attentive."

Still cautious, La Perouse and his party armed themselves well before setting off in four boats for shore, but safeguards proved unnecessary, as they came face-to-face with only peaceful Hawaiians, about 120 in number. Thinking European customs ridiculous, he declined to claim Maui for King Louis XVI of France. The islanders ceremoniously presented him with two pigs, the admiral reciprocating with some medals, hatchets and pieces of iron.

On a brief reconnaissance, La Perouse visited four small villages, each consisting of 10 to 12 thatched houses, and then reboarded his ship. His executive officer reported that during La Perouse's absence on shore, a chief had visited the ship and sold a cape, red helmet, mats, objects made of feathers and shells, and additional food supplies, including another 100 pigs, which the sailors somehow managed to stuff into their crowded shipboard pens.

Frustrated by the lack of a safe harbor, and bolstered by provisions, La Perouse set sail on that same day, never to return. La Perouse's fleeting three hours as Maui's first visitor have been honored by the renaming of the beautiful Keone'ō'io as La Perouse Bay.

A drawing by John Webber, 1779, showing Pacific explorer Captain James Cook receiving honors at Kealakekua, island of Hawai'i. This scene occurred in the same year Cook became the first Westerner to view Maui's majesty.

Admiral Jean-Francois de Galaup, Comte de La Perouse. La Perouse became the first Westerner to set foot on Maui when he landed at Keone'ō'io, near Mākena, in 1786.

Comte de La Perouse's two ships, the Astrolabe and the Boussole, off Maui.

METCALF AND THE OLOWALU MASSACRE

Tragedy followed in the wake of Simon Metcalf, captain of the American merchantman *Eleanora* - tragedy for the Hawaiians with whom he had contact, and ultimately for the commander himself.

Metcalf anchored off the southern coast of East Maui in early 1790 in search of food. In the still of the night, a Hawaiian named Kaōpuiki and a few accomplices stole a small boat, valuable for its nails and other metal, and, in the process, killed the sailor on watch. In retaliation, Metcalf fired on innocent Hawaiians in a trading canoe and on shore and, before departing, set fire to the village itself, leaving death and destruction behind.

But the worst was yet to come. Metcalf found out that Kaōpuiki lived in Olowalu and, therefore, directed his ship along the Maui coastline. Once there, his rage intensified when a promise to return the sailor's body resulted in two thighbones, stripped of flesh. As a ploy, Metcalf assured the natives of further peaceful trading, enticing 200 canoes from Olowalu, Lahaina, Ukumehame, Kāʻanapali and

Lānaʻi, many filled with parents who had brought their children to view the foreign ship. Among them was a chief who had promised to return the missing boat. Coming aboard with only the keel, he nevertheless asked for a promised reward. Metcalf responded, "I will now give the reward they little expect."

The captain placed a kapu, or taboo, on one side of the ship, crowding the canoes starboard. Once positioned, Metcalf gave the command, and the sailors opened fire at point-blank range. More than 100 Hawaiians died and another 150 were seriously wounded, as Metcalf personally supervised the carnage from his post on deck. Simon Metcalf then callously sailed away unharmed and unrepentant from what has been termed the Olowalu Massacre.

Shortly thereafter, however, he paid dearly for his inhumanity. Metcalf's 18-year-old son Thomas served as captain of the ship *Fair American*, the *Eleanora's* companion until a storm separated them. Unaware of his father's heinous acts and also ignorant of the *Eleanora's* anchorage nearby, Thomas sailed to Kawaihae on the island of Hawaiʻi.

During the previous winter Simon Metcalf had outraged many on this same island, particularly a chief named Kameʻeiamoku, whom he had flogged. Kameʻeiamoku, seeking revenge, murdered the next white men he met, which ironically was Captain Thomas Metcalf and the crew of the *Fair American*. Only one man named Isaac Davis survived.

On the same day of this disaster, John Young, an officer of the *Eleanora*, happened to be ashore nearby and was therefore aware of the incident. Fearing further violence, Hawaiians prevented him from joining his ship in order to keep word from reaching the elder Metcalf. As a result, Metcalf departed, ignorant of his son's fate.

Both Young and Davis, capable men with foreign skills, became advisors to the ambitious young chief Kamehameha. With their assistance and the arms available from the *Fair American*, Kamehameha turned the tide of history by defeating the warriors of the powerful Maui king, Kahekili, and establishing a unified Hawaiian Islands.

Hawaiians in the Olowalu area.   In 1790, Captain Simon Metcalf massacred more than 100 Hawaiians in this vicinity.

SANDALWOOD AND WHALING

Traders quickly saw financial potential in the newly discovered Hawaiian Islands. In the 1790s, ships sailing from the Pacific Northwest to China stopped in the islands for provisions and, at the same time, topped off cargoes of furs with Hawai'i's prized sandalwood, so valued by the Chinese for its fragrance. At that time, sandalwood was the only major commodity that the ali'i, or rulers, could use to attain coveted foreign goods such as ships, guns, furniture, and clothing.

Abundant stands of sandalwood flourished in Maui's mountains, but no amount could have satisfied the chiefs' voracious appetite for consumer goods. Massive cutting continued despite ever-diminishing forests. The final blow to the trade occurred in 1824, when Kamehameha III and his chiefs required subjects to make annual tax payments in sandalwood, at the same time allowing them to cut a certain amount for themselves. This doomed the sandalwood forests. Just five years later the trade was nearly at an end. Even with over a century and a half of rest, sandalwood has never recovered. Very few trees prevail on Maui today.

Destined to take over sandalwood's economic importance, the North Pacific whaling trade commenced in 1819 and expanded rapidly. Only two ports in the kingdom, Honolulu and Lahaina, provided suitable anchorages and adequate resources for the New England-based whaling ships, which required reprovisioning with food, water and firewood each spring and fall.

When the ships were in the roadstead, Lahaina bustled. In the peak year of 1846, 429 arrived in Lahaina, far surpassing Honolulu's total of 167. More than 100 vessels crammed Lahaina Roads at the same time in one record-breaking season.

Although Lahaina was the sole port on Maui capable of accommodating whaling ships, the boom affected the entire island. Hawaiians in rural areas supplied produce, meat, and firewood to the Lahaina market. The American whalers' appetite for Irish potatoes led to extensive cultivation in Kula, and the white potato became a significant reason whalers preferred Lahaina over Honolulu.

Unlike the brief contacts made by sandalwood traders, whaling vessels resided in port four to five months a year. Although such a long presence boosted business, it caused a profusion of other problems. Drunkenness and prostitution were rampant. This sinful behavior distressed Maui Governor Hoapili, a Christian convert, so he forbade both around 1826. For a period of 12 years, rum-drinking and prostitution were rare and numbers of ship arrivals fewer. However, with Hoapili's death, Lahaina again bloomed as a center of vice and debauchery.

Whaling began to decline in the 1850s due to the scarcity of whales and the subsequent loss of ships to the Civil War effort. The death knell to the industry, however, was the drilling of the first commercially successful oil well in Pennsylvania in 1859, as petroleum proved to be a better and more cheaply produced fuel than whale oil.

The demise of sandalwood trading and whaling marked the end of a staggering transition for Hawai'i, not just economically, but also culturally, for these economic activities delivered the outside world to Maui's shores, provoking a radical shift from Hawaiian to Western ways.

Whalers conquering their giant prey in the North Pacific. In Lahaina's peak year, 1846, the roadstead hosted 429 ships for rest and reprovisioning.

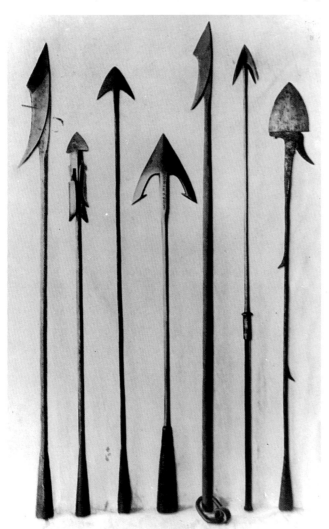

Whaling implements. Whaling replaced sandalwood as Hawai'i's trading commodity, starting in the 1820s.

KA'AHUMANU - POWERFUL QUEEN

Six feet tall, bold, fiery and beautiful, Ka'ahumanu has no equal in Hawai'i's feminist history. Her wisdom and strength guided the islands in a period of major transition for the Hawaiian people, and her actions profoundly affected the course of Hawaiian history.

Ka'ahumanu's birth was, much like her life, entangled in political intrigue and turmoil. Her mother Nāmāhana, born of high rank in the lineage of Maui chiefs, married rival chief Ke'eaumoku from the island of Hawai'i, thus giving him the advantages of her rank and her lands in central Maui. Maui's ruler, Kahekili, considering this a threat to his power, attacked Nāmāhana and Ke'eaumoku and their retinue at Waihe'e, chased them to Moloka'i and, finally, to Ka'uiki point at Hāna. There, in a small cave, Ka'ahumanu was born in 1777. Asserting the baby's rights to Maui lineage, Ka'ahumanu's family named her after their foe, Kahekilinui'ahumanu. The continued pressures of war forced her family to relocate to the island of Hawai'i when Ka'ahumanu was still a baby.

Ka'ahumanu married Kamehameha I, Hawai'i's most celebrated ruler, when she was in her early teens and he was in his 30s, and she soon became his favorite. A handsome woman, she enhanced her appearance in the Hawaiian way by tattooing her legs, hand and tongue. The royal couple spent long hours together, talking, smoking pipes and surfing. More importantly, Kamehameha carefully listened to the counsel of this strong-willed and uncommonly intelligent woman throughout the turbulent years of his ascendancy and rule.

In 1802, Kamehameha moved his family, chiefs, and fighting forces to Lahaina for a prolonged stay in preparation for war against Kaua'i. While there, he built the first western-style house in the islands for his beloved Ka'ahumanu. The house, built out of red bricks dried in the sun of Lahaina, contained four rooms in its two stories.

After Kamehameha I died in 1819, Ka'ahumanu declared herself kuhina nui, or co-ruler, with the new young king, Liholiho, also known as Kamehameha II. Greatly disturbed by the restrictions of Hawaiian religion, she persuaded Liholiho to break the kapus, or taboos, an act which unintentionally cleared the way for the arrival of the Christian missionaries one year later. The missionaries taught her to read, and she eventually accepted their religious faith as hers.

In 1824 while in Lahaina, Ka'ahumanu thought she was dying. In an effort to help her people before she died, she proclaimed a code of law for the island of Maui, prohibiting murder, theft, gambling, and the profaning of the Sabbath. These laws, though generally unenforced, were the first in the Hawaiian Islands.

Laws were needed, for there was little order in the kingdom. After an English sea captain bought an unwilling mission girl from Lahaina named Leoiki for a season's companionship, Lahaina chiefs, influenced by missionary William Richards, placed a kapu on further such transactions. As a result, angry and unruly sailors formed a mob and attacked Richards at his home.

Ka'ahumanu, distressed over this incident and by other violence that ensued, placed the weight of her authority behind the kapu. In order to protect the town of Lahaina from cannon attack, she claimed the ten gold doubloons paid for Leoiki and used it to build a fort, personally supervising its construction.

From the time of Kamehameha II's departure for England in 1823 until her death in 1832, Ka'ahumanu essentially ruled the kingdom, for Liholiho died abroad, and his brother Kauikeaouli, or Kamehameha III, was only 12 years old in 1825, when he was proclaimed king.

We are reminded of Ka'ahumanu's legacy on Maui by the historic Ka'ahumanu Church, built in Wailuku in 1876; Ka'ahumanu Highway, Kahului's major thoroughfare; and the ultimate honor of our time, the Ka'ahumanu Shopping Center.

A young Queen Ka'ahumanu. Hāna-born Ka'ahumanu, Kamehameha's favorite wife, exerted vast influence in the governing of the kingdom for many years, many of them spent in Lahaina.

KEŌPŪOLANI, KAUIKEAOULI AND NĀHI'ENA'ENA
DIVINE ALI'I

Heartache and despair plagued the lives of Princess Nāhi'ena'ena and her brother, Kauikeaouli, for these privileged royalty, perhaps more than any Hawaiians in history, were caught in a lethal crossfire between old traditions and Western ways.

Hawaiians considered them divine. Their exalted status came, not through the bloodline of their father Kamehameha I, but through their mother Keōpūolani, the highest ranking woman in all Hawai'i. Keōpūolani possessed such high status that Kamehameha himself could only enter her presence naked and with his head lowered.

Born in Wailuku, the nine-year-old Keōpūolani and her family fled to Moloka'i in fear at the time of Kamehameha's fierce assault on 'Īao Valley. Shortly thereafter, Kamehameha claimed her for himself because of the sacred mana, or supernatural power, which she possessed. When she was old enough, he married her. Although Kamehameha had nearly 20 other wives, Keōpūolani's children were the undisputed successors to his kingdom.

Keōpūolani's divine status forced her to live as a recluse and to observe other strict kapus. Rebelling against the severe restrictions placed upon her, she insisted on challenging tradition and kept her daughter Nāhi'ena'ena at her side. She also advised her oldest son, Liholiho, to break the eating kapus, and welcomed the first Christian missionaries to O'ahu.

After Kamehameha's death in 1819, Liholiho assumed rule as Kamehameha II. Four years later, after Keōpūolani's second husband, Hoapili, was named governor of Maui, she moved with her two younger children from the increasingly complex court life in Honolulu to the sleepy village of Lahaina. She escorted Maui's first missionaries, William Richards and Charles Stewart, on the return trip to her home island.

When she became fatally ill, Keōpūolani entrusted the care of Nāhi'ena'ena, age 8, and Kauikeaouli, age 10, to Hoapili, a devoted Christian, and the Lahaina missionaries Richards and Stewart. But many older chiefs surrounding the children, particularly Governor Boki of O'ahu, staunchly supported traditional Hawaiian practices. With these opposing influences, the young royals vacillated between the pressures of ancient customs, which told them they were sacred, and new teachings which told them to be humble. The most critical conflict arose from the Hawaiian expectation that the brother and sister would marry and produce the rightful heir to the kingdom.

On the death of Liholiho in 1825 after a turbulent and indulgent reign, 12-year-old Kauikeaouli moved to Honolulu to assume the throne as Kamehameha III. He missed his close companion Nāhi'ena'ena, and would often summon his sister from Lahaina to his side for parties and ceremonies. At the age of 19, unable to handle the conflicts of his life, he went on a prolonged and dissolute drinking spree.

During this period, Kauikeaouli once again sought his sister's company. Fearing Christian disapproval, she refused. The day after this rebuff, he surrendered to despair and attempted suicide. His physical recovery was rapid, and within two months the strongly attached brother and sister were married. The mission's worst fear was realized. The chiefs of the royal court, influenced by the missionaries, denied the marriage's validity and sent Nāhi'ena'ena back to Maui. There, she fell into despondency and drank heavily.

Pressured by the mission, she married the young chief Leleiōhoku in Waine'e Church (now called Waiola) in 1836. The same year she bore a short-lived child, who was said to have been fathered by Kauikeaouli. A few months later, 20-year-old Nāhi'ena'ena died from the lingering effects of childbirth.

Kauikeaouli remained faithful to his sister. He filled a handsomely furnished and light-filled mausoleum with Nāhi'ena'ena's satin slippers, silk cape and other keepsakes. For years after her death he reverently marked the anniversary with a visit to this tomb in Lahaina.

Nāhi'ena'ena's death stabilized Kauikeaouli, enabling him to turn his attention to the serious problems of his young nation. During the 30 years of his reign, King Kamehameha III inaugurated many critical reforms, including toleration of diverse religions, reforms of taxation and land, the elimination of the national debt, and the establishment of the executive branch of the government. The longest reigning monarch Hawai'i ever had, Kauikeaouli died in 1854 at the age of 41.

Around 1860, Keōpūolani and Nāhi'ena'ena were reburied together in Lāhaina at the Waine'e Church cemetery. However, in death as it was in life, the brother and sister remain separated. Kauikeaouli rests in Honolulu.

Nāhi'ena'ena as a young girl with kahili and cape, trappings of her high status. Divine by birth, Nāhi'ena'ena spent her short life torn between Western and Hawaiian ways.

William Richards, about 1843. Richards, Maui's first missionary, was Kamehameha III's chief political advisor.

Kauikeaouli, or Kamehameha III, during his 30-year reign. Kauikeaouli inaugurated many critical governmental reforms during the years he resided in Lahaina.

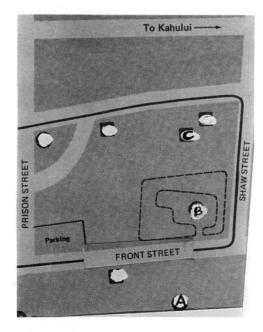

A. Site of Hale Piula or iron-roof house, a large two-story stone building built, though never completed, in the late 1830s as a palace for Kauikeaouli. Kauikeaouli, valuing the traditional Hawaiian lifestyle, preferred to sleep in a small thatched hut nearby. The stones from this house are imbedded in the historic Lahaina Courthouse. B. The location of a small island named Moku'ula, which was centered in a pond destroyed in 1918. Kauikeaouli built a mausoleum for Nāhi'ena'ena on Moku'ula. C. Waine'e Church cemetery, the final resting place for Keōpūolani, Nāhi'ena'ena and William Richards.

MISSIONARIES - A QUEST FOR SOULS

The debauchery in Lahaina was even worse than the dissipation in Honolulu in the 1820s. Drunkards, gamblers and fornicators abounded. The Reverend William Richards faced a fertile missionary field when he arrived on Maui with Reverend Charles Stewart in 1823 to "make men of every class good, wise and happy."

In 1838, after an eventful career at the Lahaina mission during which he translated almost a third of the Bible into Hawaiian, Richards left to become chaplain, teacher and translator to Kamehameha III, focusing on the teaching of politics and government to the chiefs and native scholars. As a result, Richards' students composed a declaration of rights in 1839, followed by Hawai'i's first constitution, promulgated in 1840. In 1842, as a representative of the king, he met with world leaders and secured American, French and British recognition of Hawaiian independence.

Over the following five decades, the nondenominational American Board of Commissioners for Foreign Missions dispatched a total of 37 missionaries to the four base stations on Maui - Lahaina, Lahainaluna, Wailuku and Hāna - not counting wives who labored alongside their husbands. New England Congregationalists formed the majority of the American Board, but on Maui, so many missionaries were Presbyterian that the local church association was called the Presbytery of Maui.

Reverend Jonathan Green, one of Richards' fellow religious laborers in the early years, established a station at Wailuku in 1832 and three years later founded the Central Maui Female Seminary. An ardent abolitionist, he later broke with the American Board over the issue of slavery and, as a result, independently organized Makawao Union and Po'okela churches.

The Reverends Daniel Conde and Mark Ives founded Maui's most remote mission station at Hāna in 1837. These missionaries faced transportation challenges not experienced by others, for, depending on sea conditions, a trip between Wailuku and Hāna could take from 6 to 56 hours. Nonetheless, the work at Hāna progressed with the enthusiastic support of the community. Conde constructed Wānanalua, Hāna's first church, from materials dismantled from a Hawaiian heiau, or temple.

Another of Maui's notable missionaries, the Reverend Lorrin Andrews, guided Lahainaluna as its first principal and became an accomplished Hawaiian translator. After leaving the American Board over what he perceived as a vacillating stand on slavery, he worked as a printer and eventually presided as the first Associate Justice of the Supreme Court of Hawai'i.

Also a prominent clergyman, the Reverend William Patterson Alexander spent 41 years in Lahaina and Wailuku, teaching, translating, and preaching. In 1863, he instituted the Theological School at Wailuku, which prepared Hawaiian men as pastors and evangelists.

Not all missionaries were ordained ministers, however, nor were they all white men. Betsey Stockton, a former slave, taught at Lahaina. Fellow educator Maria Ogden spent almost 30 years at both Lahaina and Wailuku, instructing Hawaiian children in reading and writing. The third woman to come independently as a missionary to Maui, Lydia Brown, spent five years at Wailuku, teaching native girls how to spin and weave Maui-grown cotton and wool.

Isolated mission stations required toilers with diverse skills. The board sent Edward Bailey as a teacher, but he also served as an agriculturist, physician, architect, engineer, businessman, botanist, surveyor, poet, musician, and artist during his years at Wailuku. Dwight Baldwin utilized both his medical and religious training in his 35 years at Lahaina. Without Baldwin, innumerable lives would have been lost in a disastrous smallpox epidemic in 1853. Saving Hawaiian spiritual lives, on the other hand, required healing through the Bible, a task fulfilled by printer Edmund Rogers.

The missionaries felt dismay when the "idolatrous" Roman Catholic Church dared to encroach on Protestantism's monopoly. Fathers Barnabe Castan and Modest Favens, and Brother Jean Marie Gabriac formed the first official Catholic mission on Maui in 1846.

But the invasion had begun earlier, for, when these three religious pioneers arrived in Lahaina, they found nearly 4,000 Hawaiians already converted to the faith. Hawaiian laypersons, principally a man named Helio Koaeloa, had introduced and zealously spread Catholicism since the late 1830s. Called the "Apostle of Maui," Helio succeeded despite the Protestants' stern prohibition against attendance at Catholic gatherings and the opposition of local authorities.

In one notable incident in 1843, the Protestant mission at Hāna notified the police that a small group of defiant Catholic women were congregating for prayer at Kahikinui. The police dutifully arrested them, tied them to each other with sennit, and marched them eastward toward Wailuku, 90 miles away. As word was passed along the route, other converts asked to be tethered to their fellow believers and joined the procession along Hāna's coast, dressed in their lei-bedecked Sunday best. By the time they reached Wailuku a month later, their numbers had risen to over 100. The judge, seeing the futility of prosecuting such a large group, dismissed the charges.

Despite Protestant persecution, Catholicism prevailed. The first formal mission, named for Our Lady of Victory, constructed Lahaina's landmark Maria Lanakila Church in 1858. By 1927, 28 Catholic churches stretched from Kīpahulu to Kahakuloa.

The Mormons followed just a few paces behind in the race for Hawaiian souls. In 1851, Elder George Q. Cannon founded the first Hawaiian branch of the Church of Jesus Christ of Latter Day Saints in the village of Kealahou near Pūlehu, followed weeks later by branches at Keʻanae, Wailua, Waianu and Honomanū. While living in Wailuku, Elder Cannon, with the help of Judge Jonatana Napela and others, translated the *Book of Mormon* into the Hawaiian language.

Collectively, these religions triumphed in their quest for the souls of Hawaiians. By 1853, almost every Hawaiian was a member of some church. Forty years later, despite continued efforts by the Protestant church, the number of Mormons and Catholics combined outnumbered Protestant church members six to one.

The Wailuku mission station with members of the Bailey family in the 1840s.

Reverend William Patterson Alexander and Mary Alexander. Reverend Alexander, considered an eloquent preacher and admired scholar, spent most of his adult life as a teacher and a linguist in Lahaina and Wailuku.

Maria Ogden about 1852. One of three women to serve on Maui independently as missionaries, Maria Ogden spent nearly 30 years as a teacher in Lahaina and Wailuku.

Reverend Louis D. Maigret. On a visit to Lahaina in 1841, Father Maigret offered the first mass ever celebrated on Maui, five years before the arrival of the formal Catholic mission.

Pūlehu chapel, Kula, and Mormon worshippers, 1880s. This chapel was built at the site of the founding of the Church of Jesus Christ of Latter Day Saints in Hawai'i.

(top) Jonathan and Asenath Green in the 1860s. Reverend Green established the Wailuku mission station, the Central Maui Female Seminary and both Makawao Union and Poʻokela churches.
(bottom) Dwight and Charlotte Baldwin during their residence at Lahaina, 1835-1870. Reverend Baldwin was not only a minister, but a physician and an educator.

PALAPALA - WESTERN EDUCATION

What was the use of preaching about the Bible if Hawaiians couldn't read it? It was obvious to the missionaries that schooling was a necessary route to salvation.

And Hawaiians were eager learners. Chiefs demanded to be taught first, but soon adult commoners and then children sought the palapala, or book learning. Heeding this call, Betsey Stockton founded the first school for commoners in the kingdom at Lahaina in 1824. Others proliferated and, within two years, 8,000 students attended almost 200 island schools, conducted either outdoors or in thatched huts.

Demand for instruction outstripped the supply of teachers, so in 1831, Maui's missionaries founded Lahainaluna High School as a teacher training center, a remarkable accomplishment for a time when no such schools existed west of the Rockies. Reverend Lorrin Andrews, Lahainaluna's principal and sole instructor in its first years, recruited "men of piety and promising talents," and gave them their initial task - to construct the first school buildings on a barren plot of land in the hills above Lahaina.

Lahainaluna, clearly the most important school in Hawai'i during the reign of Kamehameha III, produced educated Hawaiians who exerted great influence in the affairs of the nation, including a governor, ministers, teachers, lawyers, and government officials. Under the tutelage of Reverend Sheldon Dibble, Lahainaluna scholars preserved a wealth of Hawaiian cultural history. Revered native historians Samuel Kamakau and David Malo first studied, then taught, there.

Items to read were understandably in short supply. In order to meet the need for materials in the Hawaiian language, Lahainaluna installed a printing press in 1834. Within a year, this pioneering press made history by running off issue number one of *Ka Lama Hawai'i*, the first newspaper published in the kingdom. A printing house named Hale Pa'i, constructed in 1837, housed the press, which also produced textbooks, Bibles, copper engravings, maps, dictionaries and Hawai'i's first engraved paper money.

In 1835, Maui Governor Hoapili showed his support for education when he exempted all native teachers from public labor, required all children over four years old to be enrolled in school, and demanded literacy as a prerequisite for marriage. Such rules were hardly necessary. The people pursued education enthusiastically, pushing the literacy rate to a level higher than in New England, home of Hawai'i's missionaries.

In order to educate Hawaiian girls in the domestic arts and to provide future wives for the scholars of Lahainaluna, the Reverend Jonathan Green established Wailuku Female Seminary as a boarding school in 1835. The girls, aged four to ten, spent five to six hours a day in work and prayer, plus two hours in school study. This regimen, plus separation from their families, proved enfeebling to the small free-spirits, and several died. As a result, their alarmed guardians lightened demands. Edward Bailey continued Reverend Green's work, making improvements to the school complex and experimenting with crops such as apricots, lemons, corn and beans. Despite this effort, the school was abandoned in 1858.

Three years later, Reverend and Mrs. Claudius B. Andrews purchased a piece of land above Makawao for a "home school," dedicated to building character and to developing "fine Hawaiian womanhood." First called the East Maui Female Seminary, the school was later renamed Mauna'olu Seminary. After Mauna'olu burned down for the second time in 1898, it was rebuilt at a lower elevation between Makawao and Pā'ia. The seminary continued to educate Hawaiian girls through the eighth grade until 1941, when the military took over the facilities for wartime use.

Upon the arrival of Roman Catholicism in the 1840s, the priests instituted a policy of founding a school along with every church or chapel. As a result, tiny one or two-room schools nestled in almost every village throughout the island. Kaupō, for example, had two schools, one in the village and one called a mountain school. While most of these early schools eventually either closed or were consolidated, Sacred Hearts School and Saint Anthony School survived. Saint Anthony expanded its offerings to high school level in 1939. Saint Joseph School in Makawao is not a remnant of early Catholic education, having been founded in 1945.

A potential turning point in Hawaiian education occurred at the turn of the century, when authorities favored Lahainaluna as the site for a college of agriculture and mechanical arts. If these plans had been adopted, Lahaina would be the site of the University of Hawai'i today.

As it turned out, Lahainaluna endured as a vocational school open only to boys, leaving the island without general education beyond the eighth grade. In order to meet this need, Maui High School opened in Hāmākuapoko in 1913, attracting students from far-flung areas who arrived by train to pursue their educations. Additional demands for high school education prompted the establishment of Baldwin and Hāna High schools, the first classes graduating in 1939 and 1941, respectively. The desire for vocational training in central Maui led to the construction of the Maui Vocational School in 1931.

In the course of time, Maui Vocational School developed into Maui Community College, a two-year liberal arts and vocational campus. Following a period as a college, Mauna'olu still resides in its beautiful hillside location, providing education and refuge through social programs. Although all but one of the buildings of the Wailuku Female Seminary are gone, the grounds graciously host the original Green/Bailey home used as Maui Historical Society's museum. And Maui's most famous educational institution, Lahainaluna, remains unique, not only because it is one of the only public boarding high schools in the nation, but because its faculty and students deeply value its Hawaiian traditions.

The East Maui Female Seminary, later named Mauna'olu, 1880s. From 1861 until 1941, Mauna'olu educated Hawaiian girls through the eighth grade.

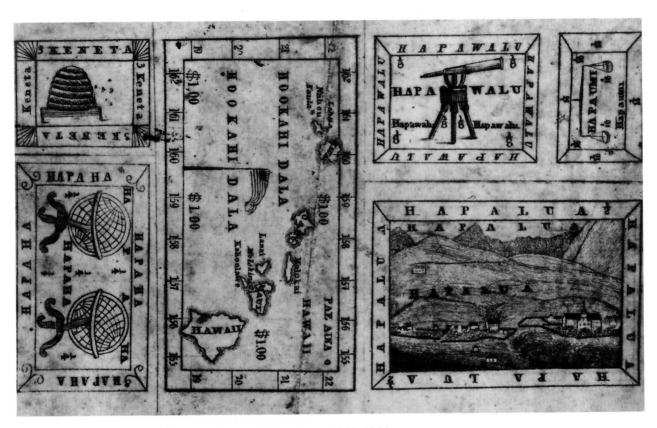

Money printed from engraved copper plates at Lahainaluna, 1843-1844.

An early illustration of Lahainaluna sketched by Edward Bailey in the 1840s and engraved by students. Lahainaluna High School was founded in 1831 as a teacher training center for promising young Hawaiian men.

Students and teacher at the Saint Anthony Boys' School in school print shop, 1924.

The student body and teachers of Honokahua School, 1920s.

BARTIMEUS AND MALO - HAWAIIAN SCHOLARS

Deformed, diseased and often numbed by the narcotic 'awa, a Maui native named Pua'aiki also faced the challenge of blindness. These obstacles did not prevent him from becoming one of the most extraordinary Hawaiians in history.

Born in Waikapū, probably about 1785, his mother tried unsuccessfully to kill him at birth, and he grew up neglected and despised. To support himself and his love of 'awa, he used his tiny, malformed body and his skill in a frenzied style of hula as a hired buffoon in the chiefs' court. As a result, he came into contact with the first Christian missionaries on O'ahu.

Converted and fervent, he returned to Maui to spread the word of God, even before the arrival of the first foreign missionaries to Maui in 1823. Over the next 20 years, he was baptized Bartimeus at Lahaina in the kingdom's first ceremony; ministered in Lahaina, Hilo, Wailuku, Kahikinui, and Honua'ula; and, a year prior to his death, became the first formally licensed Hawaiian preacher.

Bartimeus earned another remarkable distinction, that of "the most eloquent speaker in the nation." Having never read the Bible, its precise words were fixed in his memory, as was nearly every sermon he heard. An uncommonly creative thinker, he would speak until his audience "would seem electrified, and hang upon his lips with admiration." Bartimeus, the "Blind Preacher of Maui," died in 1843 in Wailuku, as greatly revered as he had been once reviled.

David Malo was a scholar of a different sort. He, too, was converted to Christianity as a young man, learned to read, and soon accumulated all the books written in the Hawaiian language. In 1831, at the age of 38, he entered newly opened Lahainaluna High School and graduated four years later.

Malo, along with fellow Lahainaluna students John 'Ī'ī, Boaz Mahune and Timothy Ha'alilio, provided guidance to Kamehameha III at a crucial time in the development of the nation. They drafted the declaration of rights of 1839 (a seminal work called the Hawaiian Magna Carta), and the next year produced the first constitution, laying the basis of law for the kingdom.

Government was only one area of accomplishment for Malo. Through his family, who was connected to the chief's court on the island of Hawai'i, he had access to the history, traditions, legends and myths of the Hawaiian people. Fortunately for us today, he took what had been in his keen memory and preserved it in *Mo'olelo Hawai'i*, now titled *Hawaiian Antiquities*. He further applied his intense energy and intellect to religion, becoming a licensed preacher in 1852. Malo spent the last year of his life ministering at Kalepolepo and Kēōkea.

Malo is honored each spring when Lahainaluna invites the community to David Malo Day, an event renowned for its Hawaiian food, games and entertainment. Twice a year the students of Lahainaluna visit Malo's gravesite on nearby Pa'upa'u, known as Mount Ball, to refurbish the giant L visible for miles around Lahaina, and to remember Malo with leis and songs.

Malo authored a striking prophecy relating to Hawaiian destiny in 1837, "If a big wave comes in, large and unfamiliar fishes will come from the dark ocean, and when they see the small fishes of the shallows they will eat them up." Malo saw clearly the wave of the future.

An engraving of David Malo, historian, minister, teacher, and shaper of Hawaiian government.

A sketch of Bartimeus printed by the American Tract Society. Known as the "Blind Preacher of Maui," Bartimeus became the first formally licensed Hawaiian minister in 1842.

HAWAIIANS - A CHANGING WORLD

Western contact with native Hawaiians proved catastrophic. A contemporary estimate places the population on Maui at the time of Hawai'i's discovery in 1778 at 124,000. By the time the missionaries arrived 45 years later, however, the community had been tragically reduced by half, and by the 1870s (after limited immigration by Caucasians and Chinese), Maui's population bottomed out at 12,000. A number of factors caused this appalling decrease, but the most devastating was the introduction of Western diseases previously unknown to an isolated, vigorous populace.

Before contact, the densest native populations resided in West Maui, Nā Wai 'Ehā (Wailuku, Waiehu, Waihe'e, Waikapū), Kahakuloa, Ko'olau, (the northeastern coast), and Hāna. All areas except Lahaina were decimated. As a commercial center, Lahaina attracted people from throughout Maui, as well as off-island, and, therefore, actually increased in population. The port of Lahaina, unfortunately, also acted as a gateway for disease.

Hawaiians first departed from a self-sufficient native economy when the chiefs' desire for Western goods forced commoners into gathering sandalwood. Later, Hawaiians seized opportunities offered by the whaling trade and either signed on as seamen, or provisioned whaling vessels with firewood, meat, salt and vegetables. Native farmers earned fortunes growing white potatoes for both whalers and California gold miners.

Countless Hawaiians lost their land use rights as the result of the Great Mahele in 1848, which established a system of private land ownership. As a consequence, some Hawaiians signed on as laborers for Hawai'i's infant sugar industry. The work did not appeal to the independent Hawaiians, and many left, although a few remained as overseers and skilled laborers. The developing ranching and shipping industries, on the other hand, attracted numerous Hawaiians. Fortunately, not all Hawaiians were landless. Those that retained their lands continued in agriculture, and native fishermen harvested the ocean's bounty.

The missionaries Christianized and educated Hawaiians and, thereafter, Hawaiians constituted the majority of preachers and teachers. After the development of constitutional government, Hawaiians filled newly defined roles in the leadership of the nation, as legislators and judges, and in other government posts.

Although Hawaiians were unable to prevent the rise in political power of the American planters and the ultimate overthrow of the monarchy, they retaliated by consolidating in support of the Home Rule Party, whose motto was "Hawai'i for the Hawaiians." Home Rulers elected Mauian Robert Wilcox as the territory's first delegate to Congress in 1900 and swept the local elections of 1903. Although the party's success was short-lived, Hawaiians continued to wield strength in local politics. Outstanding amongst Hawaiian politicians, Samuel E. Kalama provided leadership on Maui for the first 30 years of the century as Territorial Representative, Senator and Chairman of the Board of Supervisors.

In 1920, the United States Congress passed the Hawaiian Homes Commission Act in order to provide agricultural tracts for landless Hawaiians. On Maui, the Hawaiian Homes Commission set aside land at Waiehu, Paukūkalo, Kula and Kahikinui. Regrettably, after all these years, many Hawaiians languish on a list awaiting the fulfillment of this promise.

Into the 1930s, Hawaiians grew taro and other subsistence crops in rural areas, particularly Honokōhau, Kahakuloa, Waihe'e, Ke'anae, and Wailua Iki. The Hāna area persisted as a Hawaiian enclave perpetuating traditional pursuits. In more populated areas, organizations such as Hawaiian Civic Clubs, Hale o nā Ali'i, the Order of Kamehameha, and the Maui Hawaiian Woman's Club kept Hawaiian culture alive.

Despite these efforts, Americanization marched onward. The practice of ancient traditions and arts diminished and the Hawaiian language was heard less and less. In recognition of this decline, several Mossman Hawaiian Schools taught crafts and language islandwide beginning in the early 1930s. Some of the last practitioners of tapa and mat making in Hawai'i, living in Hāna, taught classes. Hawaiian language speakers continued to teach on a small scale through the 1940s, and lauhala weaving developed into a modest industry.

These efforts were not enough, however, and knowledge of the old ways continued to dwindle. Fortunately, they did not die, and in the last two decades, Maui awakened to a Hawaiian Renaissance of music, dance, sports, religion, and political activism.

The 1990 census counted 12,350 full and part-Hawaiians on Maui. As the island moves ever faster into today's complex world, efforts must be extended by all to value and preserve Hawaiians' special insights, experience and skills, for Hawaiians are the heart of the community.

Hawaiian baby eating poi out of a calabash. The number of Hawaiians declined disastrously after the introduction of Westerners and their diseases in the 1800s.

Hawaiian girls in front of East Maui waterfall, near Hāna, 1890s.

Hawaiian girl, 1900-1910.

Sam Kalama, Territorial legislator and Chairman of the Board of Supervisors from 1902 until 1933.

Charles Keahi on bass and others entertain children at Kamehameha III School in the 1930s.

A Hawaiian family in front of a pili grass house at Kaupō in the 1890s. Few Hawaiians lived in native residences after the turn of the century.

HULA - A STRUGGLE TO SURVIVE

Master hula dancers held positions of high honor in ancient Hawai'i, for their art and its rituals were vital to the fabric of society. Far more than just a diversion, the dance was interwoven with religion, poetry, music, and drama.

Men, women and children rendered hula in a wide variety of styles, but the missionaries did not discriminate - they condemned all renditions. In 1823, missionary William Ellis reacted to a hula he observed in Lahaina, "Six women, fantastically dressed in yellow tapas, crowned with garlands of flowers...began their dance. Their movements were slow, and though not always graceful, exhibited nothing offensive to modest propriety....The music ceased; the dancers sat down;...I preached to the surrounding multitude with special reference to their former idolatrous dance, and the vicious customs connected therewith...."

There is no question that certain dances were suggestive and therefore quite popular with boisterous whalers on shore leave in Lahaina. In an effort to regulate such hula, commercial performances required licenses, which were available only for the whaling centers of Lahaina and Honolulu.

Fortunately, missionaries and their followers did not totally silence the sounds of the native dance. Hula schools in all Maui districts kept traditions alive despite official disapproval. An informant in 1864 complained, "There is much hula dancing at Halehaku...the police should watch at the place mentioned, because these people are doing it all the time."

King Kalākaua, after attaining the throne in the 1870s, openly promoted the hula, inviting dancers from all the islands to his court to teach and to perform. Hula continued to blossom under the reign of Queen Lili'uokalani, but upon her overthrow, the hula was again suppressed. Traditional hula remained underground, perpetuated by small groups meeting in homes, particularly on the neighbor islands.

It was not the traditional hula that flourished in the early part of the twentieth century. In its stead, a modernized hula captivated carnival and tourist audiences. The "respectable" community did not have the same appreciation. In 1916, the Maui County Fair and Racing Association, by unanimous vote, banned an E. K. Fernandez hula troupe from the first Maui County Fair.

And yet, just five short years later, the Maui County Fair did showcase hula, although this time the Maui Hawaiian Woman's Club offered a program of authentic dances. Spectators considered the entertainment novel, as it had been so long since the dances had been publicly performed.

The controversy continued to flame. One beholder described the hula provided to Maui tourists in the 1920s as "disgusting," while another portrayed what he had seen as "pretty, charming, dainty and artistic."

Hula hit Hollywood in the 1930s, and Maui was not exempt from the mania. Miss Rita Lum Ho's "piquant Hawaiian beauty and graceful dancing" won her the title of Miss Maui in a Hollywood Hula Contest held at the ʻĪao Theater. No doubt her skirt of shimmering violet cellophane helped to clinch the win. While Miss Lum Ho never made it to Hollywood, other Maui dancers, such as 'Iwalani Gaspar and Leilani Iaea, made the big time dancing on the Mainland.

Local hula troupes multiplied. Ten entertained the visiting United States Navy fleet in 1938. The military-packed island during World War II provided eager audiences for many additional troupes that charmed audiences at U.S.O. shows.

Hula, however, was not performed by professional troupes just for visitors' entertainment. Being able to hula gave a decided advantage to politicians on the campaign trail. Partygoers at lū'aus and other social functions who could dance were easily induced on stage. Local people of all nationalities enjoyed watching, as well as dancing, the hula. Large crowds showed their enthusiasm at hula 'ūnikis, or graduations, demonstrating that Maui would not let old customs die.

Hula has survived on Maui thanks to a dedicated lineage of kumu hula, or hula teachers. Kamawa'e and Niuola'a, two of the greatest hula masters of the 19th century, were followed by Kauhai Likua, Alice Keawekāne (Mahi) Garner, Helen Apo Hanu, Ida Pakulani Long, Elizabeth Lum Ho, Harriet Stibbard and many others. Maui is particularly indebted to Emma Farden Sharpe, who devoted over 50 years of her life to the perpetuation of Hawaiian dance.

Enthusiasm for the study of hula as an expression of Hawaiian culture remains high in contemporary Maui and is matched by the appreciation of audiences islandwide.

Maui dancers posing, 1930s.

Four hula maidens pose for a formal studio portrait in the Kalākaua era, 1880s.

Hula great Emma Farden Sharpe (in back row in light attire) and her hula hālau performing in a USO show during World War II.

A drawing of male dancers made by John Webber, circa 1780.

Hula dancers entertaining on Maui, 1930s.

SURFING AND CANOEING - ANCIENT PASTIMES

On days of good surf, Maui's seaside villages would be vacant, for Hawaiians highly valued sports, and surfing most of all.

Ali'i, or chiefs, excelled at surfing, as did many commoners. Both men and women mastered wave-riding skills, enjoying not only the thrill of the ride, but also prestige. Adults relied upon long, narrow boards, rugged outrigger canoes or their bodies alone to speed them through the surf, while children joined in the fun on banana trunks.

Nineteen ancient Maui surfing spots have been identified at Waihe'e, Waiehu, Wailuku, Hāna Bay, Mokulau and Lahaina, although undoubtedly more existed. Missionary Charles Stewart remarked on what he observed at Lahaina in 1823, "It is a daily amusement at all times, but the more terrific the surf, the more delightful the pastime to those skillful in the management of the boards...hundreds at a time have been occupied in this way for hours together."

Queen Ka'ahumanu herself loved to surf Lahaina's waters. Ironically, her conversion to Christianity was a force in the suppression of surfing, as missionaries considered surfing frivolous. Surfing was also suspect because it fostered gambling, promoted the intermingling of scantily dressed men and women, and encouraged sexual freedom. Missionary pressure, along with the deterioration of traditional life that occurred after the arrival of foreigners, ensured surfing's decline.

By 1854, surfing had almost disappeared. Lahaina was the only place in Hawai'i where enthusiasm for the sport remained, and even there it was on the downturn. Few surfers remained to challenge the waves at the turn of the century.

A germ of interest infected Maui in the early 1930s on the north shore, resulting in the formation of the Ho'okipa Surfriding Club in 1936, with all of 11 boards in use. The fever spread rapidly, however, and in the next year, boardsurfing was added to the Alexander House Settlement islandwide sports program, with competitions a feature on Kamehameha Day. Slowly, but surely, surfers returned to Maui's beaches.

Canoes amused Hawaiians, not only in surfing, but also in the sport of racing, and served vital functions in fishing and in fighting wars. Canoes had brought Polynesians to settle in the distant Hawaiian Islands and, thereafter, moved sojourners from island to island and village to village. It is believed there was one canoe for every 20 to 30 people.

Hawaiians were strong and skilled paddlers. Depending on weather, wind direction and current, it would take a canoe from 6 to 56 hours to go between Hāna Bay and Wailuku. Although canoes had served Hawaiians well for centuries, little time elapsed after contact with the outside world before Western vessels undermined their use. By the mid-1800s, an inter-island crossing by canoe was unusual.

The missionaries frowned on canoe racing because of its attendant gambling, and the sport faded. Canoeing in a modern style was revived on Maui at the same time as surfing. During the 1937 Kamehameha Day races, the Kahului Surfboard and Canoe Club defeated seven other teams to claim victory at Kahului Harbor. One year later, four Waikīkī beachboys delighted Mauians by travelling from O'ahu to the Maui County Fair via outrigger canoe.

Despite this reawakening, interest in canoeing was still limited. It wasn't until the late 1940s that Kamehameha Day and Aloha Week activities included racing. During the next two decades interest in canoe racing expanded, although slowly.

Canoeing and surfing today have regained much of the renown they once received in ancient Hawai'i. These ancient sports have evolved, flourished, and added a contemporary variation - windsurfing. Ho'okipa, the same beach that led Maui's surfing revival, now claims fame as the world's top windsurfing location.

Surfing at Lahaina, the only site in Hawai'i where enthusiasm for surfing remained in the latter part of the 19th century.

Harry Robello, upper right, and Chick Daniels, bottom second from left, two of the four Waikīkī beach boys who travelled to the Maui County Fair via outrigger canoe in 1938.

Surfriding At Hookipa Gains Favor

The Hookipa Surfriders club, with a membership of 21 boys and girls, is a thriving new organization which meets every Sunday at Hookipa park. Swimming and surf riding are the principal interests of the club, but it is also a social organization.

Club members feel that the surfing in the water off Hookipa park is just as enjoyable as the sport at Waikiki.

Among those who have been surfing recently, according to the club paper, Nalu Hai Aloha O Hookipa Park, are Eddie Chong Kee, Lorna Jacobs, Maia Alapai, Felix Uchimura, Pearl Jacobs, Teruo Uchimura, Dorothy Chong Kee, Lei Emmsely, Johnny Garcia, Don Lee, Sonny Kaiakamanu, Sadao Kusunoki, Joe Alapai, Kunio Matsui, Ernest Ku and Manabu Tanaka.

Maui News *article, September 2, 1936.*

Canoe club members carrying canoe to the beach at Kahului, 1970s.

"Uncle Boogie" Wainui (standing at left), long-time coach and leader in the sport of canoeing on Maui, with his crew on Moloka'i, 1952.

Canoe shed, Hāna, 1931. Rare photo of a traditionally constructed canoe shed in use.

Outrigger canoes on the beach. Canoe racing in modern style revived on Maui in 1937.

LILI‘UOKALANI AND KALĀKAUA - BELOVED MONARCHS

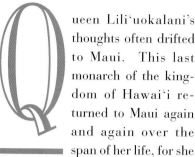Queen Lili‘uokalani's thoughts often drifted to Maui. This last monarch of the kingdom of Hawai‘i returned to Maui again and again over the span of her life, for she felt "great regard and genuine affection for Maui and its people." The sentiment was mutual.

One social visit as a young princess was particularly memorable. During the passage from O‘ahu to Maui, handsome Prince William Lunalilo, later to be king, asked her to marry him. On a romantic stroll along a Lahaina beach, the 18-year-old Lili‘uokalani accepted.

Unfortunately for the youthful couple, the engagement led to problems in royal circles and, in time, was broken. Lili‘uokalani eventually married a less-dynamic American named John Owen Dominis, who was later appointed Governor of Maui, as well as O‘ahu.

Lili‘uokalani's ties to Maui further tightened in 1874, when she accompanied her brother Kalākaua, the new Hawaiian monarch, on a formal tour of his island nation. The first Maui stop on the itinerary was Lahaina, Kalākaua's childhood home. An array of canoes lit by torches sailed to meet the royal party as they approached West Maui. The sound of Hawaiian music wafting from the welcoming fleet saturated the night air. Shoreline bonfires as far as the eye could see greeted the entourage. The brightness of Lahaina's streets, ablaze with kukui

torches, matched the fervor of its residents' welcome.

On a later stop on the tour, Kalākaua and his huge retinue landed at Mākena, where they were received by throngs of admiring subjects. Eighty torchbearers, accompanied by singers, dancers, and attendants carrying kahilis, or royal feathered standards, respectfully escorted the king's carriage on the five-mile uphill journey to ‘Ulupalakua's Rose Ranch. Captain Makee, owner of the ranch, provided entertainment lavish enough for any king. Drinking, dancing and card playing went on until early hours, followed by excursions throughout the plantation and the rose-covered grounds during the day.

Kalākaua did not need an official reason to enjoy Maui, however. During several subsequent holidays spent at his friend Makee's luxurious estate, he displayed the convivial nature that had earned him the nickname, the "Merrie Monarch." On trips to Maui, Kalākaua and his family also favored the beauty and people of Hāna, relaxing often at a veranda-rimmed seaside residence which he maintained eight miles from the village.

Following royal custom, Lili‘uokalani made two official Maui tours, one as heir apparent and one as the newly crowned queen. Each time, her subjects, both Hawaiian and foreign, showed their abundant aloha for her by honoring her with lū‘aus as she travelled throughout the island. At one stop, she was hosted by her friend and supporter,

industrialist Henry P. Baldwin, at his estate in Ha‘ikū. Lili‘uokalani arrived there in a carriage drawn by a pair of spirited horses. When she alighted, a murmur of approval went through the guests. She presented a regal image dressed in a long-trained black gown encircled with the longest golden ‘ilima leis that anyone there had ever seen.

To the dismay of her loyal subjects, Lili‘uokalani's reign was short-lived. Hawaiians suffered intensely with both anger and grief when their queen was deposed in 1893 by American businessmen, but few more so than the firebrand from Maui, Robert Wilcox. In her defense, he led an unsuccessful counter-revolution in 1895. This rebellion resulted in his being condemned to death, a sentence later commuted.

In honor of their former queen, the first Territorial Senate in 1901 voted to give the newly formed county, consisting of Maui, Moloka‘i, Lāna‘i and Kaho‘olawe, the name Lili‘uokalani County. Nevertheless, the more traditional name of Maui eventually prevailed.

Lili‘uokalani continued to visit Maui, not formally, yet no less royally. As she travelled from Kahului to Wailuku in 1903, an observer described her cortege as "a striking affair, the carriages being decked with leis, and accompanied by gaily dressed lady outriders."

On another visit in 1906, a mass of moving humanity tried to catch a glimpse of their beloved queen as her ship approached the wharf at Lahaina. Upon landing, the royal party proceeded with difficulty through the multitude to their accommodations at the nearby Pioneer Hotel.

Lahaina's climate lured Lili'uokalani back the same year for an extended stay. She called on Lahainaluna and, hearing of the reputation of poi-throwing students, requested a demonstration. A pickle jar placed boldly in front of the queen faced a poi thrower ten to 12 feet away. The apprehensive audience, no one breathing, viewed the successful filling of the pickle jar with not a drop of poi sullying the queen's regal countenance. Lili'uokalani later hosted a Christmas Day lū'au and dance for scores of her loyal supporters, a highlight of her months-long holiday.

Lili'uokalani journeyed across the channel just a few more times before her death in 1917. Maui reacted to the announcement of her passing with shock and sorrow. Steamers leaving for the funeral on O'ahu were crowded to the guardrails with Mauians who loved her and whom she had loved.

King Kalākaua in Hāna, circa 1879.

Princess Lili'uokalani prior to her departure for England in 1887.

Kalākaua in Wailuku, possibly during his official tour of the island after taking office as king in 1874.

Sixth from left, Liliʻuokalani on porch of August Unna residence at Hāna in 1883.

SUGAR - KING OF ISLAND INDUSTRY

Wispy tassels of flowering cane have long streamed in Maui's breezes, for sugar grew wild in ancient Maui. Its existence at the time of Western contact piqued foreign interest in its commercial potential. Two Chinese named Ahung and Atai in Wailuku, and a Spaniard named Antone Catalina in Waikapū initiated the first known sugar operations on Maui in the 1820s.

Although many early ventures failed, overall the industry prospered. The most important technological breakthrough in the infant Hawaiian sugar industry occurred at the East Maui Plantation in 1851, when a centrifuge that separated sugar from molasses was introduced.

By 1862, four plantations on Maui (Brewer, in Makawao/Hāli'imaile; East Maui at Kaluanui; Ha'ikū; and Makee at 'Ulupalakua) produced 650 tons of sugar, close to 50 percent of Hawai'i's total output. In that same year, three more plantations at Waikapū, Hāna and Lahaina looked forward to harvesting their first crops.

Over time, growers proliferated, particularly after the United States Reciprocity Treaty of 1876 gave Hawai'i the advantage of duty-free sugar. Sugar fields in Hāmoa, Spreckelsville, Kīpahulu, Kīhei, Huelo, Nāhiku, Olowalu, Pā'ia, Hāmākuapoko, Keāhua, Kahului, Pu'unēnē, Waihe'e and Wailuku claimed space on the sugar industry

map. Even Kū'au had its own venture in the 1870s, whimsically named the J. M. Alexander Seaside Farm. Due to business failures and mergers, the number of companies decreased to 11 by 1900, a figure further reduced to 6 by 1929.

While the number of companies decreased, sugar production did not. The Hawaiian Commercial & Sugar Company alone produced 75,000 tons of sugar in 1929 from 7,600 harvested acres. HC&S has ranked as the largest and most profitable sugar operation in Hawai'i for decades.

In the 1920s and 1930s, HC&S housed 7,000 workers and their families in 26 camps scattered throughout the plantation. Four public schools, three Japanese language schools, ten churches, a hospital, 12 day nurseries, three theaters, a gymnasium, and a swimming pool existed within plantation boundaries. The company also maintained a dairy, a meat market and several general stores.

Second in size to HC&S, the Maui Agricultural Company formed from the consolidation of the Ha'ikū Sugar Company and the Pā'ia Plantation in 1903. During the 1920s, the company put 50,000 tons of sugar, as well as 20,000 tons of pineapple, on America's tables, and a bounty of beef in local iceboxes. Like HC&S and other sugar companies of the time, Maui Agricultural Company provided housing, plus a network of recreational, commercial, and social services, for its workforce. As a novel response to World War I

shortages, the company ran its equipment and vehicles on fuel produced in its molasses alcohol distillery, the first to be constructed in the United States. In 1948, Maui Agricultural Company merged with HC&S, under whose name the sugar cultivation and Pā'ia mill operations continue.

Ever since 1862, the Pioneer Mill Company has planted and milled cane in the Lahaina area. Pioneer Mill's sugar acreage and harvests equaled those of Maui Agricultural Company with more than 45,000 tons produced annually from 5,000 harvested acres. More than 10,000 acres planted in cane were irrigated by 80 million gallons of water daily from three pumping stations, 12 artesian wells, and the Honokōhau Ditch. Olowalu Sugar Company, the smallest of the six plantations extant in 1929, bordered the sugar acreage of the Pioneer Mill Company and was acquired by them in 1931.

Wailuku Sugar, another company with a long history, commenced business in 1862 and expanded 22 years later through acquisition of the Waihe'e and Waikapū plantations. The medium-sized Wailuku Sugar produced 20,000 tons each year in the 1920s. The company continued to produce sugar until the 1980s, when a name change to Wailuku Agribusiness reflected a new focus on diversified agriculture.

Ka'elekū Sugar Company, the fifth surviving sugar company in the 1920s, had purchased the Hāna

Plantation Company in 1905. Each year the company produced more than 6,000 tons of sugar from 1,500 acres spread from Kaʻelekū to Puʻuiki. Sugar operations ceased in Hāna in the mid-1940s.

Although the sugar industry no longer dominates Maui, it maintains a strong economic, social and physical presence. The view of the vast fields of waving green cane blanketing the island, so beautiful as seen from the air, is visual testimony to sugar's continuing significance on Maui.

Maui field workers alongside flume, 1920.

The Wailuku Sugar Company mill in the 1890s.

Maui sugar workers loading cane into railroad car, central Maui, 1930s.

(Above) Celebration upon the completion of the Waiheʻe ditch, 1882. The Waiheʻe ditch, built by Claus Spreckels, was the first to bring water to central Maui from the West Maui Mountains.

Hāmākuapoko Mill, used by the Haiʻkū Sugar Company from 1884-1905. This mill was replaced by Maui Agricultural Company's Pāʻia mill.

The Olowalu Sugar Company mill between 1870 and 1890.

Hawaiian Commercial & Sugar Company Camp 8 Store, around 1918.

BALDWIN AND SPRECKELS - SUGAR BARONS

Although Henry Perrine Baldwin and Claus Spreckels were vastly different men, they both deserve the title of sugar baron. In the final analysis, however, Maui sugar planter and capitalist Baldwin rises above Spreckels as one of the most powerful influences in the development of industrial Hawai'i.

Born in Lahaina to missionary parents in 1842, 21-year-old Baldwin began his career in the sugar business at his brother Dwight's West Maui enterprise. In 1869, he formed a historic partnership with Samuel T. Alexander when they jointly purchased the first tract of land for their eventual Pā'ia Plantation. The eventual outgrowth of this partnership was the forging of the firm Alexander & Baldwin, destined to be one of the most important commercial organizations in Hawai'i.

In 1876, Alexander and Baldwin realized that they required substantially more water for the survival of their East Maui sugar operation. With an eye to the future, they ambitiously, and some said foolishly, began the construction of a system of open ditches, iron pipes and tunnels through 17 miles of rain forest on the windward slopes of Haleakalā. Innumerable obstacles confronted the creation of the Hāmākua ditch, as this project was called. Outstanding among them was the crossing of steep-sided Māliko Gulch. The workers refused

to drop into this deep ravine, so Henry Baldwin, although still recovering from the loss of his arm in a mill accident, grabbed a rope with one hand and swung 300 feet into the gulch. He repeated this feat every day, followed by the laborers, until the work was completed. Baldwin had a compelling reason to expedite the work, as the Hāmākua water rights would transfer to his ambitious rival Claus Spreckels if the two-year project deadline was not met.

Much to Spreckels' disappointment, the Hāmākua ditch, Hawai'i's first important irrigation project, was completed in 1878, right on schedule. The original Hāmākua ditch, although no longer used, was the first of several irrigation networks operated by the East Maui Irrigation Company that still feed Maui sugar today.

After Alexander left Hawai'i for health reasons in 1883, Baldwin took over full direction of the partnership's affairs in Hawai'i and continued in that capacity until his death in 1911. During that period, his business empire expanded. Baldwin developed his most significant acquisition, the Hawaiian Commercial & Sugar Company, into the most profitable plantation in Hawai'i.

Baldwin's interests reached beyond business, however. A fluent Hawaiian language speaker, Baldwin served in the Hawaiian legislature from 1887 to 1903. During this tempestuous period, he supported a constitutional monarchy

and accepted annexation to the United States reluctantly. In addition, Baldwin generously contributed to countless charitable causes throughout his life.

Henry Baldwin's contemporary and competitor, San Francisco sugar refiner Claus Spreckels, sailed to Hawai'i in 1876 with a vision of immense fortune to be made in duty-free sugar. With this in mind, Spreckels instituted a massive agricultural venture on Maui's barren central plain. In 1878, with King Kalākaua's help, he acquired 40,000 acres, plus water rights, and then followed Baldwin's lead by constructing his own 30-mile ditch system. The site he chose for his mill was named Spreckelsville, in his honor. Practically overnight, the Hawaiian Commercial Company, ultimately incorporated as the Hawaiian Commercial & Sugar Company, became the biggest and best-equipped plantation in the islands. It attracted even further notice by installing the first electric lights in the kingdom in 1881.

Concurrently with his development of Hawaiian Commercial Company, Spreckels and a partner garnered control of almost the entire Hawaiian sugar crop as highly successful sugar agents. King Kalākaua sought loans from Spreckels and, within a short period of time, the man known as the "Sugar King of Hawai'i" or "His Royal Saccharinity" held more than half the national debt of the kingdom.

After a falling out with

Kalākaua in the mid-1880s, Claus Spreckels returned to California. The Hawaiian Commercial & Sugar Company subsequently suffered reverses, causing Spreckels to lose financial control. The plantation was sold to Alexander & Baldwin in 1898.

Spreckels' tenure on Maui was short and his contributions are seldom remembered. On the other hand, Baldwin's descendants have perpetuated his active involvement in industry, politics and philanthropy, making Baldwin one of the most recognized names in contemporary Maui.

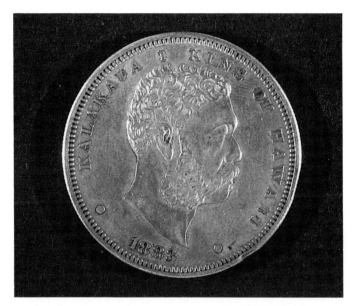

Hapahā, or quarter dollar, with the image of King Kalākaua, part of the only set of national coinage used in the kingdom, 1884-1904. Spreckels' vast wealth financed the coins.

In center, Henry P. Baldwin, with plantation assistants at the turn of the century. Baldwin distinguished himself as an industrialist and a philanthropist.

In center with beard, Claus Spreckels in front of HC&S store, 1882-1886. Spreckels maintained two stores, a large one in Kahului and a branch in Spreckelsville. The Kahului store, a rival for any store in Honolulu, did a business of about $50,000 a month in 1884.

Bridge over Māliko Gulch. This gulch gained fame, not only because Baldwin descended into it in order to complete his Hāmākua Ditch, but also because it required the building of the longest and highest bridge in the territory.

CHINESE

Only five years after La Perouse first set foot on Maui, Hawaiians confronted yet another peculiarly dressed and distinctively featured people - the Chinese. In 1791, British Captain William Douglas of the schooner *Grace* dropped off two Chinese men seeking stands of aromatic sandalwood. By 1828, two more adventurers named Ahung and Atai had founded a sugar mill in Wailuku. Shortly thereafter, other Chinese entrepreneurs opened businesses in Lahaina and grew Irish potatoes in Kula for the whaling and California Gold Rush trades.

In 1852, Maui's two sugar plantations, Brewer and East Maui, satisfied their need for labor by importing Chinese desperate for work. As pioneer sugar workers, they endured long hours, low wages, and cruel treatment. And yet, dissatisfied immigrants had nowhere to turn, as the repressive contracts to which they were bound prevented them from either quitting or seeking redress. Anyone breaking his contract faced punishment meted out by island courts.

Fortunately, plantation contracts did not last forever and, after expiration, most laborers either returned to China or turned to various other occupations. Former field workers, as well as others who immigrated independently, opened businesses such as the Lamb Sung store in Wailuku, the Tuck Sang saloon in Kula, and the Goo Lip store in Lahaina. Tong Akana, or Akana Li'ili'i as Hawaiians called him, owned and operated sugar plantations in Ha'ikū and Makawao. Other Chinese earned a living as rice, taro, or vegetable farmers, or as cattle ranchers.

Many migrated to Kula, swelling its Chinese population to 700 by the turn of the century, almost a quarter of the total Chinese population on Maui. Chinese in Kula, as well as other Maui locales, sent their children to both public and Chinese language schools and attended various Chinese churches. Some Chinese in the community frequented opium dens, while others found companionship in Chinese societies.

Chinese Tong societies formed, not only for religious and political purposes, but also for mutual aid. Members benefited from friendship and financial assistance while alive, and were assured of a proper funeral and burial at life's end. At one time, six clubhouses existed on Maui, but today the Lin Hing Society Clubhouse in Ke'anae, the Tow Yee Kwock Society in Wailuku, and the Chee Kung Tong Society clubhouse in Kīpahulu are gone, and the Chee Kung Tong building in Wailuku is in irreparable decay. Fortunately, the Wo Hing Society clubhouse in Lahaina and the Kwock Hing clubhouse in Kula have been preserved as a reminder of these important Chinese cultural institutions.

Hawai'i's most famous Chinese resident and father of the Chinese Revolution, Sun Yat Sen, first stayed on Maui as a teenager during visits to his brother Sun Mei in the 1880s. As a prosperous Kula rancher, Sun Mei enjoyed high status in the Chinese community. Because of this, Sun Yat Sen later returned to Kula to seek financial and political support for his struggles in China. When Yat Sen feared retribution because of his revolutionary activities, he sent his wife, mother and children to his brother's Kama'ole Ranch for safekeeping. The Kula Chinese backed Yat Sen's efforts in China, so, when word reached Kula that the 1912 revolution had been a success, the community burst into revelry, Chinese-style, with a boisterous parade, music and firecrackers.

After annexation to the United States in 1900, Hawai'i became bound by the Chinese Exclusion Act, which prohibited Chinese immigration. From that time, no new arrivals could replace those who departed. This law, together with frequent intermarriage, decreased the number of full Chinese in the community. Although few in number, the Chinese have played an important part in the development of modern Maui. Edward Fooksin "Eddie" Tam, a popular musician and Chairman of the Board of Supervisors from 1948 until 1966, and Andrew Wong, the first Chinese judge west of the Rocky Mountains, are notable examples of community leadership.

In 1989, island Chinese established a Sun Yat Sen Park, honoring Chinese immigration as well as Kula's celebrated son, not far from his brother's former Kula home.

Everyday reminders of Maui's rich Chinese heritage include delectable pork-filled buns called manapua, the salty-sweet tang of li hing mui, a community fondness for fireworks, and the intriguing oriental merchandise at Ah Fook's Super Market. And when you find just the perfect fruit-picking pole in a crowded and creaking bamboo forest, thank the Chinese!

Chinese woman on Maui in formal wear, with baby, 1920s.

A Chinese funeral wending its way down Market Street into Happy Valley, Wailuku, 1890s.

Edward Fooksin "Eddie" Tam, Chairman of the Board of Supervisors from 1948 until 1966, with Supervisor Joe Bulgo.

Henry S. Fong's Store and Service Station, Kēōkea, 1930s. Fong himself is at work, accompanied by his wife, Violet, at right, and customers Henry and Anna Hew.

Fourth from right, Sun Yat Sen on Maui, circa 1905. Also pictured are Sun's wife, children and mother, as well as his brother Sun Mei and family.

Chinese bazaar on Maui, 1910.

PACIFIC ISLANDERS

Sugar planters looked to island inhabitants for their next group of recruits. Unfortunately for the hopeful sugar industry, the arrival of three ethnic groups, collectively called South Sea Islanders or Pacific Islanders, did little to fill the void left by the departure of the Chinese. The Islanders included immigrants from the New Hebrides (now called Vanuatu), the Gilbert Islands (now part of Kiribati), and Tonga, all of whom arrived in Hawai'i before 1885.

Hāna Plantation became one of the first sugar operations in the kingdom to hire Pacific Islanders when they imported two distinct groups - Melanesians from the New Hebrides and Micronesians from the Gilbert Islands. In 1881, 30 Gilbertese and 19 New Hebrideans were on the payroll. Hawaiians nicknamed the Gilbertese lewalewa, meaning dangling earrings, as the Islanders were fond of suspending assorted items from their ear lobes, anything from flowers to pipes. Mistakenly, many applied the name lewalewa to New Hebrideans as well. The two small groups suffered from cultural and language isolation, not only from each other, but also from the wider Polynesian and European community, and did not become permanent settlers.

Another group, a colony of 80 consisting of Gilbert Islanders and a few Tongans, lived in Lahaina until 1903. While in Lahaina, the Pacific Islanders developed a prosperous business in hat making and mat work. Reverend Martin Lutera, a native Hawaiian and former missionary to the Gilbert Islands, ministered to the Lahaina group. The Islanders worshipped in a church they built themselves with the aid of Lutera. When they returned home after their extended stay, the church was torn down. As they were considered a sober and industrious people, the community lamented their departure.

An immigrant from the Gilbert Islands hired to work at the Hāna Plantation, 1883.

PORTUGUESE

Emigration from Portugal to Hawai'i seemed like a win-win situation for both nations. Because the United States Reciprocity Treaty of 1876 eliminated tariffs on sugar, the demand for labor bloomed. And, due to the appalling decrease in native Hawaiians, withering villages and towns needed revival. The Portuguese seemed likely prospects to fulfill both of these needs. Poverty in their homeland provided impetus to leave, and, unlike the Chinese, they stood ready to adopt a new homeland. As a result, within 22 years of their first recruitment in 1878, the Portuguese constituted 12 percent of the Territory's population.

The vast majority of Portuguese recruited for plantations throughout Maui found positions as skilled or semi-skilled workers, or as overseers. Almost three times as many Portuguese worked as lunas, or overseers, as any other ethnic group. In 1915, Portuguese lunas averaged $2.24 a day, considerably better than field hands.

Despite their relatively privileged status, many Portuguese left the employ of the plantations after 1900 to enter business, the skilled trades and other occupations. Having come from the small, crowded islands of Madeira and the Azores, the Portuguese highly valued land ownership, motivating many to settle in the upcountry areas of Kula and Makawao to farm and to ranch.

Like other ethnic groups, the Portuguese banded together for mutual benefit. Entrepreneurs organized the Kaupakalua Wine and Liquor Company in 1905, offering stock only to their fellow countrymen. The Portuguese formed clubs and organizations for social, educational, and financial purposes, such as the San Antonio Society, the Lusitana Society, the Maui Portuguese Civic Association, and the Minerva Society.

Devout Portuguese attended Catholic churches throughout the island. A remarkable Catholic church in Kula is a conspicuous example of Portuguese dedication to religion. The octagonal Holy Ghost Church, built in 1894 by Portuguese parishioners and paid for by the auctioning of cattle donated by Portuguese ranchers, remains today as an extraordinary landmark housing the finest 19th century ecclesiastical art in Hawai'i.

The Portuguese quickly took to politics and law. Starting with the election of William J. Coelho to the Territorial Legislature of 1905 and highlighted by Elmer F. Cravalho's rise to Statewide power from the 1950s to the 1980s, Maui Portuguese have made their political presence felt. Cyrus Nils Tavares, son of longtime Territorial legislator, Antone Ferreira Tavares, garnered acclaim as Hawai'i's first permanent federal judge and one of its legal giants.

Mauians today enthusiastically seek pao doce, or sweet bread, on grocery shelves islandwide and, when extraordinarily lucky, savor homemade loaves browned in the few remaining traditional ovens. Bean soup made with spicy Portuguese sausage rounds out a popular menu, along with sugar doughnuts known as malasadas. Residents of all ethnic backgrounds experience Portuguese food and customs at the Holy Ghost religious and community festival yearly in Kula. And, any day of the year, islanders appreciate the Portuguese influence through the ever-present sounds of the 'ukulele.

Former mayor Hannibal Tavares surrounded by his sisters, left to right, Edith, Helen, Margaret and Sophie.

A group of Portuguese sugar workers at Hāna, 1883.

Portuguese (and a few Hawaiian) parishioners in Catholic processional, 1908.

Territorial Senate, 1927, with Senator Antone F. Tavares in right foreground. Tavares served with Maui Senator Harold W. Rice, second from left in the front row.

JAPANESE

As the sugar industry burgeoned, so did its need for labor. The expense of Portuguese immigration caused planters to focus once again on Asia, this time on Japan. The first officially sanctioned group of Japanese reached Maui in 1895 and, 30 short years later, nearly 20,000 lived on the island, a whopping 40 percent of the population!

Maui's early Japanese laborers strained under a ponderous workload 26 days a month, 10 to 12 hours a day, all for the meager sum of $9 a month, if male, but only $6, if female. Not surprisingly, within a month of the arrival of Maui's first Japanese immigrants, disillusioned workers at Pā'ia protested their grueling labor conditions by refusing to work. Although Maui's paternalistic plantations improved working and living conditions over time, plantation life remained arduous. As strenuous as conditions on Maui may have been, the situation elsewhere was sometimes worse. The Japanese consul in the 1920s encouraged dissatisfied laborers from other islands to move to Maui for relatively better treatment.

Not all immigrants from Japan spoke Japanese. Some were Okinawans, who not only spoke their own language, but had a different appearance. The first Okinawans arrived in Hawai'i five years later than the pioneering Japanese from other prefectures. By 1918, over 2,500 Okinawans resided on the island, most of them sugar workers in Pā'ia, Pu'unēnē, and Lahaina. Their numbers expanded enough by 1931 to support their own newspaper, titled *Shinjidai*. Today Okinawans compose 15 percent of the Japanese population.

Although many Japanese remained as sugar workers, others quit the plantation for opportunities in business or diversified agriculture. Eight Japanese commercial photographers operated studios as early as 1909 and, before 1920, five Japanese language newspapers published on the island. Japanese stores and hotels proliferated, such as the M. Ichiki Stores in Wailuku and Lahaina, Noda Fish Market in Kahului, Akinoya Hotel in Wailuku, and Wakida Hotel in Lahaina. Some Japanese grew pineapple on leased land, and one company, the Pā'uwela-based Maui Pineapple Company, was Japanese-owned. Families such as the Hashimotos excelled in fruit growing and truck farming, while others fished commercially.

Along with meager material possessions, immigrants journeying from Japan carried a strict work ethic and a respect for education. Parents expected children to succeed as Americans in the public schools and, at the same time, retain their cultural heritage. For this reason, the earliest immigrants founded Japanese language schools on Maui. By 1932, 29 schools enrolled nearly 6,000. These schools taught children in large communities, as well as small ones such as Kīhei, Pa'uwela, and Waihe'e.

By the early 1930s, approximately 1,500 Hawaii-born Japanese American citizens filled the voter registration rolls on Maui. The first Japanese candidates for office, including long-term politician Toshio Ansai, won elections in that same decade, but political strength as an ethnic block did not materialize until 1944, when the Japanese American-dominated Democratic party took over Maui politics. In the 1950s, Pā'ia-born Patsy Takemoto Mink embarked on her rise to political prominence, resulting in multiple terms in the United States Congress.

Japanese influence on Maui remains strong in diverse facets of island life. Buddhist temples in each community invite residents of all religions to their summer O-Bon festivals. No local resident would consider entering a house with shoes on, and few lack skill with hashi, or chopsticks. The Japanese are also responsible for dozens of revered foods, including a local version of sukiyaki called hekka, sushi, saimin, tempura and the perennial children's favorite, shave ice. And what could be more tantalizing on a lazy day at the beach than Hawai'i's premier aroma - teriyaki sizzling on a hibachi.

Japanese child on Maui in the 1920s.

Left to right: Yoshio Ikeda, Yosaku Shimomura, and Shigeru Shimomura, with prize ulua at Japanese Camp, Honolua, circa 1935.

Japanese sugar field workers on Maui in the 1920s. The Japanese constituted 40 percent of Maui's population during this period.

Japanese women at Honolua. These pineapple workers and their families are awaiting the distribution of mail at the plantation post office.

Maui Jodo Mission band, 1915.

Long-term politician Toshio Ansai, 1980s. Ansai first won election in 1934.

MORE EUROPEANS

Sugar managers, every one of them haole, or Caucasian, worried about Hawai'i's future. Could Hawai'i prosper if dominated by Asians? Their ethnocentric answer was no. In an effort to provide a haole backbone to the community as well as to their work force, sugar interests sought disparate groups of Europeans, namely Norwegians, Swedes, Germans, Scots, Italians, Spaniards and Russians.

Scandinavians were the first of these Europeans to reach Hawai'i, and Maui was the first island to welcome them as laborers. The bark *Beta* sailed into Mā'alaea Bay in 1881 with 228 adults and children, mostly Norwegians with some Swedes, assigned to labor in Wailuku, Ha'ikū, Hāmākuapoko, and Pā'ia. Not long after, more compatriots followed. But few stayed long, as the Scandinavians were craftsmen, artisans and city-dwellers and eventually sought better opportunities elsewhere.

Germans followed closely behind the Scandinavians. Approximately 150 Germans arrived as laborers in the 1880s and 1890s and were widely disseminated to plantations in Pā'ia, Kīpahulu and Olowalu. Independent immigration added to their numbers, but the population remained small. Germans held positions at all levels, from field workers and lunas, or overseers, to plantation managers. John Fassoth, for example, managed Kīpahulu Sugar Company. As a result, their modest numbers were disproportionate to their influence.

The Scots, on the other hand, never labored as field hands. As the only ethnic group recruited solely as managers, they presided over sugar plantations from the late 19th century. By 1905, almost two of every five plantation bosses in Hawai'i were of Scottish descent. Maui's managers sported names such as Burns, Campbell, McLeod and Campsie.

Still needful of labor, Hawai'i looked to Italy. Since the Italian government refused to permit recruitment in their country, sugar industry representatives enlisted Italian laborers fresh off the boat in New York City. A few hundred arrived on Maui from 1899 to 1900 for employment at the Spreckelsville plantation and the Kahului Railroad. Members of the group made a favorable impression within a week of their arrival when they celebrated the turn of the century by serenading a New Year's ball in Spreckelsville with songs from their home in southern Italy. More importantly, the Italians impressed their employers with the quality of their work. Much to the disappointment of sugar industry management, better opportunities lured most elsewhere within a few years.

Hopeful once again of increasing Hawai'i's European laborer pool, recruiters visited Andalusia in Spain. A few hundred Spaniards made the long journey to Maui between 1907 and 1914 to work primarily at plantations in Pu'unēnē, Pā'ia and Wailuku. Unfortunately for their hopeful sponsors, most followed the lead of the Scandinavians and Italians and left within a few years, destined for California and higher-paid employment.

Planters tried for the last time to secure Europeans as permanent residents in 1909 and 1910, when more than 50 Russian families from Poltava, Kiev and Volga landed in picturesque costume on Maui's shores for jobs in Spreckelsville, Waikapū, Lahaina, and with the Kahului Railroad Company. Like most Europeans before them, the majority emigrated to Honolulu or to the United States mainland within a short period of time. By 1929, almost no Russians remained on Maui.

Although relatively few in number, descendants of European immigrants remain on Maui, the Spanish Molina and the German Meyer families among them. Hopefully they will preserve accounts of their adventurous great-grandparents to add yet another shade to the colorful history of Maui.

Hyman J. Meyer, circa 1913. Half-German, half-Hawaiian businessman Hymie Meyer was the son of David Meyer, who immigrated around 1880.

Norwegian Johannes Johansen, around 1925. A blacksmith, Johansen and his wife Maren Helena immigrated with the first Scandinavians to arrive in Hawai'i in 1881.

Molina's Orchestra at the Grand Hotel, Wailuku, 1947. Five members of the Molina family - Joe, Dominic, Salvador, Henry and Tony - provide a Spanish base to this multicultural band. Molinas have been entertaining Maui audiences since 1935.

Spanish sugar workers, 1915.

PUERTO RICANS

Bad weather blew Puerto Ricans to Hawai'i's shores. A hurricane devastated Puerto Rico in 1899, destroying the island's economy and forcing its citizens to seek a livelihood elsewhere. The sugar industry, desiring non-Asian labor and burdened by the expense of importing Europeans, regarded Puerto Ricans as likely prospects, particularly considering their experience as agricultural workers on a tropical island.

The first group of 114 men, women and children left Puerto Rico in 1900 with high hopes. On the long train journey across America, however, fellow Spanish-speaking travellers spoke negatively of conditions in Hawai'i, provoking half of the contingent to slip away in San Francisco. Only verbal threats and physical force kept the remainder on their appointed route.

These 56 Puerto Rican immigrants, the first in the kingdom, reached Lahaina on the inter-island steamer *Lehua*, destined for employment at the Pioneer Mill. The newcomers' first impressions proved positive, as Lahaina was similar to their island in landscape and climate. Within the next year, others arrived to work at the Pā'ia and Wailuku plantations.

The Puerto Ricans, like the Portuguese, brought wives and large numbers of children, additional resources for the labor-hungry sugar industry. Workers aged 15 or older of either sex were sought for field work, but not compensated equally. Men received 50 cents for each day of a 26-day monthly work schedule that first year, while women collected only 40 cents per day, and girls earned only 35 cents.

Despite the hardships of plantation life, many Puerto Ricans stayed on Maui, keeping alive their music, dance and oral traditions. They formed Puerto Rican clubs and athletic teams and enriched the membership of local Catholic churches. The people of Puerto Rico, being of varied European, Indian and African backgrounds, commonly intermarried, so in their new homeland they easily accepted partners from Hawai'i's many races.

Most eventually left plantation work for other occupations and professions. Perhaps the best-known Puerto Ricans in Hawai'i, Mauians John and Joseph Bulgo made their mark in both business and politics. Voters elected either the father or the son to the Maui Board of Supervisors or County Council in every decade from the 1940s to the 1980s.

Maui history recorded no politicians as dynamic and dramatic as the Bulgos.

Many descendants of the early Puerto Ricans on Maui celebrate their ethnic identity through the Maui Puerto Rican Association. The Association is well known for its food booth at the Maui County Fair, where thousands of Mauians have feasted on tamale-like pasteles, rice flavored with gandule, or pigeon peas, and bacalao, or codfish, salad. And, judging by the length of the line, Puerto Rican cultural traditions are here to stay.

Puerto Rican troubador, Lahaina, early 1900s.

Sally Orta, Christina Roman, and Helen Roman, young
Puerto Rican women living in Upper Pāʻia, circa 1924.

Puerto Rican wedding, 1920s.

AFRICAN AMERICANS

Faced with growing labor unrest, sugar industry managers throughout Hawai'i considered using Americans of African descent from the southern states as another wedge in their campaign to racially divide and conquer. Nonetheless, Maui was the only island to actually tap this labor source during the wave of immigration that marked the turn of the century.

Black laborers disembarked on Maui's shores for the first time in 1901, when approximately 100 city dwellers from Tennessee arrived to work for the Wailuku Sugar Company. Two other groups from rural areas in Alabama included male recruits, along with their wives, children and a pair of Protestant ministers, all destined for Spreckelsville.

From the standpoint of the plantation managers, the Alabamans proved to be the better and more stable workers, being accustomed to agricultural labor. This opinion was reinforced when several of the Tennessee contingent walked off their jobs, thus generating labor problems rather than preventing them.

The Tennessee sugar workers were familiar with walkouts, as they had been sent in as strikebreakers shortly after their arrival to replace Hawaiians at the Wailuku railroad depot. Harmony, however, not animosity, marked this event. After a knot of Hawaiian strikers gathered to watch work proceed, one of the group suggested that they were willing to take over the loading of sugar if the Blacks would favor them with some songs. The laborers from Tennessee agreed and serenaded the Hawaiians with "My Old Kentucky Home," "Suwannee River," and "Way Down South in Dixie," interspersed with hoedowns, buck and wings, turkey trots and juba, dance steps uncommon in Hawai'i. After the impromptu concert ended, both groups genially returned to their former activities.

Unfortunately for the sugar planters, the African Americans' residency on Maui was brief. Most of the laborers, unhappy on Maui due to low wages, the high cost of food and their inability to own a home, left for Honolulu within the year.

The most notable recruit to Maui, William Francis Crockett, graduated from the University of Michigan law school in 1888. Desiring passage to Hawai'i, he signed on as a laborer, worked for two years at the Hawaiian Commercial & Sugar Company, and then distinguished himself as an attorney and judge in Wailuku. The voters of Maui elected Crockett to the 1915 Territorial House of Representatives and later sent his son Wendell to the Territorial Senate and to the County Board of Supervisors.

African Americans came to Maui independently as well, beginning with Betsey Stockton's arrival as a missionary teacher in the early 1820s. W. L. Maples contributed to the community as a doctor and drugstore owner during his 42-year residency.

Long after most of the Black sugar laborers left, the home to many of these sojourners was called Alabama Camp. As a more permanent legacy, descendants of these immigrants still contribute to Hawaiian society, including William Crockett's namesake grandson, who has followed in the family tradition as an attorney.

William F. Crockett, 1920s. An attorney, legislator and judge, Crockett arrived on Maui in 1901.

Haleakalā Ranch cowboy Benny Rollins, late 1930s.

Betsey Stockton, around 1863. Missionary Stockton arrived in Lahaina in 1823 and shortly thereafter established a school for commoners.

KOREANS

Sugar workers from Korea, a country traditionally at odds with Japan, offered a promising alternative to managers facing ever-increasing Japanese labor strength. As a consequence of recruitment aimed at racial divisiveness, between 1903 and 1905 hundreds of Koreans joined Maui's ethnic medley.

Although poverty fueled many Koreans' departure from their homeland, it was not the only impetus. Some sought a better education for themselves and their children, while others desired religious freedom. Unique among Hawai'i's immigrants, many Koreans were city dwellers, some were literate and almost all were Christian. Unlike others, Koreans represented a diverse strata of society.

Few would find the wealth they sought, as Korean field laborers received only $16 for a month's labor. Koreans labored from one end of the island to the other - at Pioneer Mill, Kīhei Plantation, Maui Agricultural Company, Kīpahulu Sugar Company, the Hāna Plantation, and Wailuku Sugar Company. The largest group of 236 worked for the Hawaiian Commercial & Sugar Company, where they comprised 10 percent of the work force in 1905.

Initially, men outnumbered women ten to one, as most Korean males dreamed of returning home one day with a fortune in their pockets, a task made more difficult by the presence of wives and children. After a number of years, however, many Korean bachelors decided to settle permanently in the islands and looked to their homeland for wives. Between 1910 and 1923, young picture brides arrived in Hawai'i to meet and marry their prospective husbands.

Major Japanese strikes on O'ahu in 1909, 1920 and 1924 lured large numbers of Koreans off-island with the opportunity to earn generous bonuses as strikebreakers. Life on O'ahu appealed to the former urbanites, so, few returned.

Most Korean immigrants brought their missionary-taught Protestant (predominantly Methodist) beliefs with them to Maui. The Congregational churches on Maui, although numerous, had very few Korean members, as they had earlier agreed to limit their missionary endeavors to the Chinese and to allow the Methodist mission to work among Koreans. In order to serve newly arrived Maui parishioners, the Hawaiian Methodist mission dispatched Reverend C. P. Hong in 1906, the first of several Koreans to minister to his people.

Small congregations worshipped throughout the island. While Koreans in some areas were fortunate to have a church such as the Korean Methodist churches in Hāna and Spreckelsville and the Korean Christian Church in upper Pā'ia, other believers practiced their faith wherever space could be found. For many Koreans, life revolved around the church. Early immigrants relied upon their minister for aid and guidance, and a great amount of social life was church-related.

Since their numbers were relatively small, Koreans associated often with other ethnic groups which encouraged rapid Americanization. First-generation Koreans were not altogether pleased with this trend. Parents attempted to pass on their language and culture to their children by requiring them to attend Korean language school, but they were largely unsuccessful.

The descendants of plantation immigrants established businesses joined the professions and influenced the development of modern Hawai'i. Dr. Ron Kwon and his father, John, a well-known educator, represent Maui well on the Hawaiian roster of notable Koreans. Attorney Kwan Hi Lim deserves special notice as the most colorful Korean from Maui, due to his experience as a motion picture and television actor.

Koreans cannot be easily identified in the island racial lineup. The curious can most easily distinguish Koreans from other Asians through reoccurring surnames, particularly the name Kim, one of the ten most common names in Hawai'i. Although seldom seen, the distinctive short jacket and long, full skirt worn by Korean women at cultural festivals is a reminder of Korean presence in contemporary island life. Mauians are most frequently reminded of Korean presence, however, when their mouths tingle with kim chee, a spicy cabbage salad, often accompanied by kalbi barbecued ribs, two of Maui's most popular taste experiences.

Spreckelsville resident Kwan Hi Lim, circa 1945.

ISLAND SON

Publicity still for attorney-turned-actor Kwan Hi Lim, 1989. Lim has had parts in numerous movies, Hawai'i Five-O and Magnum P.I .

Korean women modeling formal wear on Maui. Left to right, Ki Im Lee Kihm and Mrs. Min in women's wear, and Ho Si Lim donning men's clothing.

The congregation of the Korean Christian Church of Upper Pāʻia, about 1936.

Korean women from Pāʻia wearing traditional costume, around 1920.

FILIPINOS

The labor-hungry sugar fields and mills of Maui demanded more workers, and Filipinos fit the bill. Not only were they agricultural workers eager for self-advancement, they also could enter Hawai'i without a passport or visa. Recruiters first transported Filipinos to Maui in 1909, in response to the threat of a Japanese-led strike. After 17 short years of intense immigration, Filipinos outnumbered all other races on sugar plantations.

Filipinos initially received free passage, three years of guaranteed employment, free housing and a wage of $18 a month, the equivalent of a year's income in the Philippines. Most Filipinos taking advantage of this offer came to Maui as unmarried young men seeking money necessary to support a family in the Philippine barrio.

Although some Filipinos fulfilled this dream, many found that their wages did not stretch as far as they expected. As the last ethnic group to join the plantation, Filipinos labored at difficult menial tasks, and, as they were largely illiterate due to a recruiting policy seeking the least educated, workers held little hope of advancement. The lack of family life added to Filipino dissatisfaction. Being free to move as American nationals, Filipinos could express their discontent by departing either for the mainland or back to the Philippines, and almost half did just that.

To provide some relief for those who remained, the Filipino community developed an active social life. All-Filipino bands, such as the Hāli'imaile Camiling Tralac Orchestra, performed throughout Maui in the 1930s. Churches and hometown societies served immigrants' needs, as did cockfighting and dime-a-dance halls. Athletes organized leagues to play sipa, their native ball game, and spiritedly competed in American sports, as well. In 1928, the Japanese newspaper *Maui Record* extended its readership to the Filipino community by adding a one-page section in the Ilocano language.

Loyalty to home remained strong. Filipinos commemorated Filipino Flag Day and Philippines Commonwealth Day, but reserved special enthusiasm for Rizal Day festivities at the end of each year. Rizal Day, a two-day event of programs, parades and queen contests held in communities from Hāna to Lahaina, honored Filipino patriot Jose Rizal.

Although early arrivals were Vasayan, a dialect group from the central Philippines, by 1930 Ilocanos from the remote and crowded northern area of Luzon composed over 90 percent of Maui's Filipino population. Though women had been initially reluctant to leave the Philippines, an increasing number did so with the encouragement of the sugar industry as part of its unceasing campaign for a stable work force. Even so, during the last wave of Filipino migration, male newcomers still outnumbered women and children four to one.

Despite the departure of many unhappy immigrants, the Filipino population continued to rise as poverty in the Philippines ensured a steady arrival of replacements. It took the Depression to reverse this flow of Filipinos. In order to offset relief roles, the sugar industry provided free passage to many unemployed workers so they could return to the Philippines.

As the last to be hired on the plantations, Filipinos were hard hit by Depression layoffs. The lucky ones who retained their jobs dug deep into their own pockets to support their countrymen. In 1932, fellow Mauians donated an estimated $75,000 to Filipino relief, an amount which averaged to $6 per month per employed worker. These contributions, in combination with the practice of taking in the unemployed, feeding and clothing them, meant that Maui Filipinos supported 1,000 of their compatriots in their entirety.

Immigration resumed after World War II for the last time. In only six months of 1946, before the independence of the Philippines legally curtailed the flow, approximately 1,000 Filipinos left their homeland for Maui.

Today, Maui's Filipinos are active in business, the professions, government and the arts. Asiclo Baylon Sevilla served Maui for many decades as a businessman and community leader. In 1956, Richard Caldito became the first Filipino in Hawai'i to be elected to a county council seat. Alfred Laureta stands out as the first State cabinet-level officeholder and the first Federal judge of Filipino ancestry in the United States.

Filipinos have added their own rich texture to the local ethnic tapestry. Local residents of all backgrounds relish a noodle dish called pancit and its cousin, the savory stuffed lumpia, as well as sugar doughnuts known as cascaron. An embroidered shirt called a barong tagalog is common men's dress wear. And the graceful movements of beautifully costumed Filipina folk dancers entertain the Maui community at festivals throughout the year.

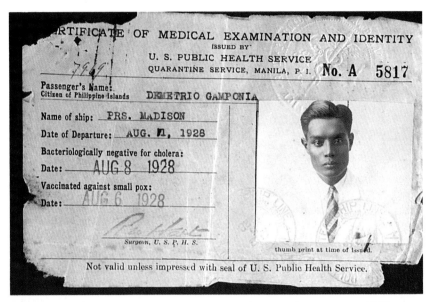

Official document accompanying immigrant Demetrio Gamponia in 1928. Unlike most Filipinos who worked in the sugar and pineapple industries, Gamponia became a businessman.

Baldwin Packers pineapple worker, Patricio Munar, circa 1940.

Filipino policemen, 1930s.

Wedding of Demetrio Gamponia and Barbara Aquilizan, circa 1946, at Wailuku. Filipino men outnumbered women four to one.

PINEAPPLE - QUEEN OF ISLAND INDUSTRY

Pineapples provide a golden hue to Maui's variegated economic history. Although the spike-topped fruit had long grown in Mākena and elsewhere, pineapple production as an economically important industry first surfaced in 1890 with successful plantings by Dwight David Baldwin in Ha'ikū. By 1920, total exports from Maui amounted to 730,000 cases, making pineapple queen consort to king sugar.

Pioneer planter D. D. Baldwin first shipped fresh fruit to the mainland in 1900, and three years later, in cooperation with his brother Henry P. Baldwin, established the Ha'ikū Fruit and Packing Company. The construction of a can-making plant and a cannery in 1904 made possible an initial pack of 1,400 cases of canned pineapple. The company, in order to provide fruit for their Ha'ikū cannery, convinced others to plant pineapple at Grove and Haleakalā ranches, as well as on hundreds of small properties in Ha'ikū, Kaupakulua and the Makawao area.

Within a few years, the Pukalani Dairy and Pineapple Company and the Japanese-owned Maui Pineapple Company of Pa'uwela were formed, both of which eventually became successful units of Ha'ikū Fruit and Packing. Not all of Ha'ikū Fruit and Packing's efforts succeeded, however. The company abandoned an attempt to grow pineapples in Hāna and Kīpahulu in 1927, despite heavy investment in the construction of a cannery and employee housing. The trailblazing concern, by then named simply Ha'ikū Pineapple Company, was sold to Hawaiian Pineapple Company in 1934. Hawaiian Pineapple closed its Maui operation only four years later.

In 1912, David Fleming founded what was later to be renamed Baldwin Packers by planting pineapple on a small section of the Honolua Ranch in West Maui. Eventually, neatly planted fields covered 2,500 acres from Māhinahina on the south to Kahakuloa on the north. The fruit, processed at a cannery at Honokahua, departed for the outside world via Kā'anapali landing. In 1922, the Territory of Hawai'i erected Māla Wharf, motivating Baldwin Packers to build a cannery close by, in Lahaina. Pioneer Mill cane cars conveniently transported pineapples to this processing plant.

A year earlier, Maui's production increased with the incorporation of the Pa'uwela Pineapple Company. A Kui'aha cannery packed fruit from independent growers in the Ha'ikū area, supplemented by company plantings in Kahakuloa. The Chicago-based Libby, McNeill & Libby took over the successful firm in 1926 and expanded its operations to Makawao.

The industry advanced yet another step when the California Packing Corporation initiated operations in Kahului in 1926, with an agreement to can fruit supplied by the recently established pineapple divisions of Haleakalā Ranch and Maui Agricultural Company. Six years later, Haleakalā Pineapple Company (Haleakalā Ranch's pineapple division) took over Maui Agricultural Company's holdings, forming a year later as the Maui Pineapple Company, headquartered at Hāli'imaile under the leadership of J. Walter Cameron. Cameron expanded the company's sphere of endeavor by purchasing California Packing Corporation. Cameron's 32 years as president and manager of Maui Pineapple earned him the admiration of the Hawaiian pineapple industry, which dubbed him the "Man of Maui and Pineapple."

All of today's pineapple roads lead to one cannery. Libby closed nearly 40 years on Maui in 1963, when it sold its cannery to Haserot Pineapple Company. The year before, Maui Pineapple Company had merged with Baldwin Packers and subsequently acquired the Haserot Pineapple Company, forming the still-competitive firm now called Maui Land and Pineapple Company.

Haʻikū Fruit and Packing Company shed, circa 1920. Brothers Dwight D. and Henry P. Baldwin founded this pioneering pineapple concern in 1903.

An identification tag, known as a bango, from the Haʻikū Fruit and Packing Company, used at plantation stores and on payday. The initials are incorrect as the P had been lost.

A pineapple worker packing fruit, 1920s.

The Honolua ditch which fed West Maui pineapple fields, 1913.

Men loading pineapple on escalator conveyor at harvest time, Hāli'imaile. These conveyors came into use during World War II, when harvesters were in short supply.

Honolua Store, late 1940s. At this time, the store, which sold merchandise to Baldwin Packers employees, lacked glass in its windows and therefore needed to be shuttered in the evening.

Hawaiian Pineapple Company label, 1930s. Hawaiian Pineapple Company, originally Haʻikū Fruit and Packing, operated only from 1934 to 1938 on Maui.

David T. Fleming, Baldwin Packers manager, and employees enjoying picnic at company park, around 1950. The site of the picnic, then sometimes called Fleming Beach, now goes by the name Kapalua Beach.

Maui Pineapple Community Association patch used by employees at Hāliʻimaile, post–World War II. The association provided recreational opportunities for Haliʻimaile workers and especially the children.

The trimming line at Maui Pineapple Company's Kahului cannery, 1960s.

Construction of California Packing Corporation's Kahului cannery, 1926.

PANIOLO COUNTRY

Wild-eyed bulls with horns up to six feet across squared off with bold and crafty cowboys called paniolos in Maui's earliest cowpunching days. Cattle ran freely after their introduction by George Vancouver in the eighteenth century, due to a kapu placed on them by Kamehameha I. By the time the ten-year kapu was lifted in 1803, cattle had spread far and wide over lava-strewn mountain range and only daredevils could catch them.

Eventually fences kept stock contained, allowing cattle-raising to burgeon into Maui's third biggest industry, behind sugar and pineapple. From 1893 until 1927, close to 1,600 brands were registered on Maui, representing operations throughout the island. Ranch sizes ranged from a few acres to the 80,000-acre 'Ulupalakua Ranch, Maui's largest.

Captain James Makee founded 'Ulupalakua as the Rose Ranch in 1856. For much of its history, 'Ulupalakua Ranch ran more than 5,000 head of cattle, annually sending 1,000 to market in Honolulu through the port of Mākena. Because Mākena lacked a deep-water wharf, this was no easy task! Transporting stock from shore to ship required paniolos on horseback to drag recalcitrant cattle by rope into the pounding surf and to swim them to a waiting longboat, where six to eight would be tethered to each side by their horns. Then the water-logged and undoubtedly perplexed cows would be rowed to a steamship, encircled by a sling, and lifted aboard for the final voyage. In addition to cattle, for many years 'Ulupalakua Ranch bred and trained many of Maui's famed polo ponies. Today 'Ulupalakua continues in cattle as well as sheep raising.

Without question, 'Ulupalakua's head cowboy Ikua Purdy deserves the title as the most renowned of Hawai'i's paniolos. After Purdy triumphed in the World's Steer Roping Championship at the 1908 Frontier Days in Wyoming, a Cheyenne news report stated that his performance, along with that of fellow Hawaiian ropers, "took the breath from the American cowboys."

Purdy emerged victorious over a five-time world champion roper and star broncobuster with Buffalo Bill's Wild West Show named Angus MacPhee. Shortly thereafter, Wyoming native MacPhee made Maui his home, earning near-legendary status in Maui paniolo history. An outstanding cattleman, he helped to pioneer the cattle-raising industry on Maui through introduction of purebred stock and the improvement of several ranches, including Raymond Ranch (later part of 'Ulupalakua Ranch) and Grove Ranch.

No less deserving of membership in Maui's ranching hall of fame, Haleakalā Ranch manager Louis von Tempsky nurtured one of Maui's largest and well-known cattle operations for 20 years at the turn of the century. His outstanding knowledge of cattle and horses, combined with his passion for the open range, enhanced his territory-wide reputation. Some say his ghost still rides those expansive pastures, keeping an eye on the land he loved.

Founded in Makawao in 1888, Haleakalā Ranch over time raised both beef and dairy cattle, and cultivated pineapple. The ranch today maintains from 4,000 to 6,000 head of beef cattle on 32,000 picturesque acres.

Ranches were also maintained by sugar and pineapple plantations, such as Pioneer Mill, Baldwin Packers, and Hawaiian Commercial & Sugar Company. Through stock raising, plantations utilized marginal land, provided meat and dairy products for employees, and furnished draft animals for plantation work.

Cattle first grazed in the Kaupō area, Maui's most remote corner, in the early 1800s. Kaupō Ranch, the outgrowth of initial ranching efforts, supplies meat to local markets to this day. The 16,000-acre Grove Ranch stretched from Ha'ikū to Makawao. Although Grove Ranch liquidated in the 1960s, two other large operations remain productive - the Hāna Ranch and the Ka'ono'ulu Ranch on the slopes of Haleakalā.

In his younger days, Ka'ono'ulu Ranch manager Harold F. "Oskie" Rice earned the epithet "the cowboy of cowboys in Hawai'i." Infatuation with both cowpunching and competition inspired George Manoa, Sr., Rice and others to form the

Maui Roping Club in 1955 and, just one year later, to sponsor the first Makawao Rodeo. Rodeo enthusiasts will long remember Rice through his gift of land for a Makawao arena, gratefully named after him.

Paniolo tradition remains vibrant on Maui. The celebrated Makawao rodeo held each Fourth of July highlights a rodeo season that showcases Hawai'i's best ropers and riders. Thousands of fans crowd Makawao's Oskie Rice Arena to admire handsome and daring cowboys and cowgirls performing hazardous feats Hawaiian style, so reminiscent of those intrepid paniolos of long ago.

Honolua Ranch land overlooking Punalau Beach, also known as Pohakupule Beach, circa 1920. Due to the expansion of pineapple on ranch lands, the Honolua herd had diminished to 450 head in 1931.

Manduke Baldwin and his crew of cowboys branding cows at Haleakalā Ranch, 1940s.

Louis and Armine von Tempsky around 1904. This famous father and daughter led an idyllic life at Haleakalā Ranch.

Kaupō cowboy, 1920s

Ka'ono'ulu Ranch manager Harold F. "Oskie" Rice, circa 1940. Rice's father, Harold W. Rice, purchased the Cornwell Ranch in 1916 and changed its name to Ka'ono'ulu.

Cowboy Willie Holomalia and horse Buster at Haleakalā Ranch, 1920s.

Haleakalā Ranch cowboys herding cows, 1940s.

Haleakalā Ranch cowboy George Manoa, Sr., early 1950s. Manoa was the first president of the Maui Roping Club.

Milk covers representing plantation, ranch and independent dairies around the island.

TRAINS AND SHIPS - ISLAND LIFELINES

Hawaiians aptly named the mammoth black machine ka'aahi, or fire wagon. Thomas H. Hobron, William Bailey and William Smith introduced the ka'aahi when they founded the Kahului and Wailuku Railroad, the first common carrier in the islands. On the railroad's opening day in 1879, a locomotive named the *Queen Emma* transported a load of sugar from Wailuku to the wharves at Kahului. Two years later, the company incorporated as the Kahului Railroad Company.

Initial success led to more demand, and, within two years of *Queen Emma's* short but historic passage, the Kahului Railroad had laid track to the mills at Spreckelsville, Lower Pā'ia and Wailuku. In 1902 and 1905, respectively, the line reached sugar mills at Pu'unēnē and Upper Pā'ia. By 1913, the Kahului Railroad extended from Pā'ia, through Hāmākuapoko, to the pineapple fields and canneries at Pa'uwela and Ha'ikū. Deep-gouged Māliko Gulch had presented a formidable obstacle to connecting these East Maui sites. This challenge resulted in the construction of the longest and highest bridge in the territory, 684 feet in length and 230 feet in height. In 1924, Kahului Railroad tracks lengthened even further, from Ha'ikū to the pineapple cannery in Kui'aha.

After the addition of the Kui'aha extension, Kahului Railroad's network amounted to 50 miles of track,

nine depots and more than 250 cars. By 1936, Kahului Railroad had reached its peak, with 443 freight cars on its roster. Cars carried not only freight, but also passengers - 55,000 climbed aboard in 1908. Students from central Maui joined the general public in 1913 as daily commuters to newly opened Maui High School in Hāmākuapoko. Kahului Railroad replaced its passenger service with a fleet of buses in the mid-1930s.

The Kahului Railroad inspired the namesake Hawaiian song and hula, "Ka'aahi Kahului," a familiar favorite in Hawai'i. Audiences smile with both recognition and pleasure upon hearing "Wuwu! Chuku chuku maila, chuku chuku maila," the sounds of Hawai'i's best-known railroad.

Although celebrated, the Kahului Railroad was not the only train in town. Beginning in the 1880s, individual sugar and pineapple plantations laid several networks of track to carry harvests from the field to their mills and canneries, as well as to transport their employees.

Famed for being the first, Kahului Railroad also bears the distinction of being Hawai'i's last. A long history of island railroads ceased when steam engine No. 12 wheezed to a stop in 1966.

On an island, a railroad can go only so far. Therefore, Kahului Railroad Company developed the harbor at Kahului in order to efficiently launch its freight to off-island destinations. Strong winds and

heavy seas beset the first docks. In an effort to subdue Mother Nature, the company built the West and East breakwaters in several stages from 1905 to 1931, utilizing in excess of 593,000 tons of rock. The territorial government took over the port facilities in 1923, the same year that Pier One was constructed. The expansion of the pineapple industry, together with hopes for increased tourism, provided the impetus for better facilities. In 1927, Pier Two replaced the 1910 vintage Claudine Wharf. At this time, the port of Kahului handled over 370,000 tons of trans-Pacific and inter-island freight. By 1944, the total volume of freight had risen to nearly a million tons.

And yet, Kahului Harbor did not always reign as the king of island shipping. Ship captains of the nineteenth century preferred Lahaina. The waters off Lahaina simmered with hundreds of ships, predominantly whalers and interisland coasters loaded with provisions gathered from all over Maui for the whaling trade. Activity in Lahaina often outpaced that of Honolulu Harbor during the whaling era. Even after whaling died, Lahaina remained active as the second most important port in the islands. But Lahaina Harbor was far from perfect; in fact, at times it was deadly perilous. A number of severe accidents after the turn of the century convinced authorities to abandon the Lahaina wharf and to replace it with a new facility at nearby Māla.

The Māla Wharf, completed in 1922, proved to be worse. Those attending its dedication suspected a serious mistake had been made when the first ship docked there rolled so heavily it knocked down posts wrapped in bunting and nearly upset tables set for the celebratory lūʻau. Thereafter, because of prevailing crosscurrents, it was necessary for large offshore vessels to ferry passengers to the wharf via motor launches. Adding to the wharf's problems, storm-driven high seas caused considerable damage in the 1940s. Māla, the white elephant of Hawaiian wharves, today offers only a dangerous perch for island anglers.

Most sugar enterprises faced major transportation obstacles in the nineteenth century. Delivering their product overland to major ports proved infeasible due to deeply-gouged gulch terrain. As a result, many plantations were forced to establish their own landings near their mills. Smaller coastal vessels handled this trade, but at a risk. Several boats were destroyed while loading sugar at precarious landings along the northeast coast.

The *Constitution*, the first steamship to serve the Hawaiian inter-island trade, crossed the channel between Oʻahu and Lahaina in 1852. Thus began a competition between steam and sail which persisted until 1910, when the last of the sailing schooners withdrew from service. The Wilder Steamship Company served all ports on the island of Maui in the latter decades of the nineteenth century until it merged with the Inter-Island Steam Navigation Company in 1905. When the *Haleakalā* was christened in 1923, it became the first of a series of modern inter-island passenger vessels. The largest vessel up to that time, the 300-passenger *Haleakalā* offered many amenities, including Irish linen and private baths for those who could afford first-class staterooms. Two years later, before air transportation had made major inroads into passenger traffic, Kahului Railroad's shipping department handled 278 steamers filled with 185,000 passengers.

In 1914, Inter-Island's regular ports of call on Maui included Lahaina, Olowalu, McGregor's Landing, Kīhei, Mākena, Nuʻu, Kaupō, Kīpahulu, Hāna, Keʻanae, Kahului and Honolua. At different times in Maui history, the shipping trade utilized other landings at Nāhiku, Māʻalaea, Kalepolepo, Māliko, Kūʻau, and Kāʻanapali.

Today's transportation technology has not completely replaced that of yesteryear. In 1970, entrepreneurs laid rail abandoned by the Kahului Railroad on a roadbed previously used by Pioneer Mill's rail system. Since that time, the Lahaina, Kāʻanapali and Pacific Rail Road has offered tourists and local folks alike a spectacularly scenic ride in passenger cars reminiscent of old Hawaiʻi. Although the vast majority of contemporary travellers choose the lower fares and speed of air travel, those desiring ease and luxury opt for the few remaining inter-island and trans-Pacific cruise ships. Alone among former isle modes of transport, ocean freight service has increased. Today Kahului Harbor handles twice the tonnage it did in the 1940s.

The SS Haleakalā *docked in Honolulu. This 300-passenger inter-island passenger vessel was christened in 1923.*

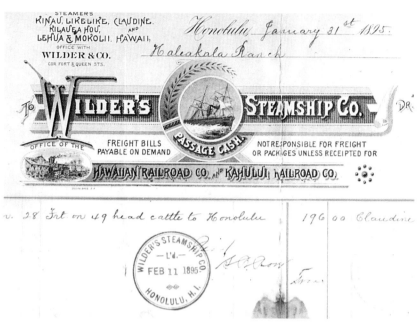

Honolulu, January 31st 1895.

Haleakala Ranch

TO **WILDER'S** STEAMSHIP CO. DR.

PASSAGE CASH

OFFICE OF THE

FREIGHT BILLS
PAYABLE ON DEMAND

NOT RESPONSIBLE FOR FREIGHT
OR PACKAGES UNLESS RECEIPTED FOR

HAWAIIAN RAILROAD CO. AND KAHULUI RAILROAD CO.

v. 28 Frt on 49 head cattle to Honolulu   196 00 Claudine

WILDER'S STEAMSHIP CO.
— L'd. —
FEB 11 1895
HONOLULU, H.I.

Wilder's Steamship Company invoice, 1895.   This company provided inter-island transportation until it merged with the Inter-Island Steam Navigation Company in 1905.

S/s "Matsonia" passing S/s "Maui" at sea.

A ship loading at Māla Wharf, 1922, with warehouse on left. This is one of the few large ships ever to dock at Māla.

Kahului Railroad invoice, 1891, reflecting the company's interests in both land and sea transportation.

Brochure touting the pleasure of visiting Maui, the Valley Isle, circa 1918.

Business card circa 1942.

Kahului Railroad stamps, 1894-1899.   Kahului Railroad was the only Hawaiian railroad to carry mail with its own stamps.

Train on Kahului pier, late 1800s.

TOURISM - A LONG ROAD

Brothels and grog shops doubled as hotels for the first wave of Maui tourists - thousands of boisterous whalers crowding Lahaina in the mid-19th century.

After the whaling boom died, visitors to Maui were uncommon. A traveller in 1880 either stayed in lodging houses such as Ford's in Wailuku, others in Lahaina and Makawao, or in private homes. As one sojourner to Lahaina put it, "The sleeping accommodation procurable by travellers who have not any introduction to private families is very inferior, and I can only repeat my former advice to tourists, that by far the best way to travel in this country is to take your own tent and camp outfit, and get a good native attendant to accompany you."

A tourist paid dearly for his discomfort. A bed in Lahaina cost 50 cents a night, which, when added to 25 to 50 cents per meal at one of three Chinese restaurants in town, and two or three dollars a day for a horse, emptied a wallet quickly. If travellers wanted to go beyond these basics for an exotic excursion, they could hire a whaleboat pulled by six men to Moloka'i for an outlay of ten dollars.

At the turn of the century, Wailuku, not Lahaina, was recognized as Maui's prime tourist destination, with three hotels handling a small tourist trade. Guests considered The Windsor, the town's principal hotel, a "charming little hostelrie." Visitors preferred Wailuku because it was a more convenient home base for ascending Haleakalā, the island's chief attraction, and for the popular four-mile horseback ride into nearby 'Iao Valley, considered the "Yosemite of Hawai'i."

Although Wailuku hosted most of Maui's tourists, Lahaina also welcomed visitors, housing them in hotels such as the Pioneer Hotel (now the Pioneer Inn), built in 1901. These hotels, however, primarily lodged travellers who were in Lahaina for business, as long and arduous trips from other sites on Maui or other islands dictated at least one night's layover.

As the century progressed, a visit to Maui continued to require lots of time, endurance, and money, so visitors were few. Those that did rise to the challenge arrived first in Honolulu after a seven-day transoceanic steamship passage from the West Coast that cost a hefty $125 for basic round-trip accommodations. They then tossed and rolled for several hours on windy and choppy seas aboard an Inter-Island Steam Navigation Company freighter-passenger ship.

At the major port of Lahaina, passengers disembarked via a rope ladder into a small swaying boat and then were rowed ashore through crashing waves. At other landings, a member of the ship's crew threw voyagers bodily to the waiting arms of a bobbing boatman, who rowed them to the wharf. Not out of danger yet, the passengers, depending on ocean conditions, risked harm once again by being heaved to the pier. Occasionally, travellers drowned attempting such precarious landings.

Once settled on shore and ready for sightseeing, the adventurer faced a rugged horse or mule ride up a long and sinuous trail to the summit of Haleakalā. Once there, the only shelter from near-freezing overnight temperatures was a shallow cave infested with fleas. Beef jerky and hard poi provided sustenance.

Realizing that harsh conditions stifled tourism, Maui eventually added creature comforts such as roads and harbors, rental cars and a rest house on Haleakalā. The Wailuku Hotel, the Maui Hotel and the Grand Hotel, all in Wailuku, as well as the Pioneer and Hāna hotels, offered decent lodging. Hoping to entice visitors to the new and improved island, national promotion touted isle attractions. Contrary to expectations, tourists did not flock to Maui - only 428 arrived in 1927.

Several factors combined to alter the Maui tourism picture dramatically. First, inter-island air transportation was launched in 1929. Pioneering passengers landed at Mā'alaea airfield aboard Sikorsky planes after a 75-minute flight from Honolulu. Over time, flights became faster, more comfortable and less expensive, due to the introduction of larger capacity DC-3s in the 1940s, and jets in the 1960s. Other significant influences came into play after World War II, when former isle-based servicemen returned in peacetime as tourists.

Per capita income rose, communication systems improved and tourist promotion intensified. Organized tours arrived in the late 1940s, though not often. When they did, a grateful community welcomed any sizeable group with an article, plus photo, in *The Maui News*.

The early 1950s were, at the time, considered boom years for neighbor-island tourism. Maui attracted over 10,000 tourists annually, although visitors could only minimally experience the island after a typical one-day, high-pressure tour around a circuit of sites. Lack of facilities kept them from lingering. In 1952, the Hotel Hāna Maui was the only hotel that catered to the tourist trade. The Maui Palms, opened in 1954 at Kahului, was a first attempt to meet this need, shortly followed by the construction of the Hotel ʻIao Needle and the Maui Hukilau Hotel.

These efforts paled in comparison to the glamour of Kāʻanapali, Hawaiʻi's first destination resort area created out of scrub land in the early 1960s. This large development contained hotels, restaurants, a shopping center and golf course, everything a visitor could ask for, all in one area. Not only did Kāʻanapali pin Maui securely on the tourist map, it set a precedent for tourism development statewide.

Investment in the promising tourist industry spread beyond Kāʻanapali. The Hale Nāpili, the Hotel Mauian, the Nāpili Kai apartment hotel and the Maui Lu blazed the trail in Nāpili and Kīhei, defining these communities as tourist areas.

Maui's luxurious accommodations of today are a far cry from that dank and dreary Haleakalā cave. Despite a vast difference in amenities, visitors of yesteryear and today have one thing in common - cherished island memories.

Welcoming a visitor to Kahului Airport, early 1950s. Trans-Pacific Airline, later named Aloha Airlines, began service to Maui in 1949.

Visitors to Maui on board ship to return to Honolulu, 1930s.

Tourist postcard, 1930s.

Tourists offloading at Kahului, 1921.

Inter-Island Airways sticker, 1930s.

Boat Day at Pier 2, Kahului, 1930s.

The Maui Hotel

Tourists' Headquarters

The starting point to all places of interest on the Island of Maui.

THE MAUI HOTEL ANNEX "Kapaniwai"

Ideally Situated in the Picturesque Iao Valley The Yosemite of Hawaii Invigorating Climate and Magnificent Scenery

THE MAUI HOTEL CO., LTD., Proprietors W. H. Field, Mgr.

Haleakala Trips Maui Headquarters Maui Hotel Co. Ltd.

What to See on the Island of Maui

MAUI, THE VALLEY ISLE, is fast becoming one of Hawaii's greatest tourist attractions. Finest auto roads of all the islands, an excellent hotel, the many wonderful scenic attractions, and the real hospitality extended to all by the Maui people has made of this wonderful island a place that few tourists neglect to visit.

HALEAKALA, "THE HOUSE OF THE SUN," the largest extinct crater in the world, with its awe-inspiring grandeur and gorgeous sunsets, is the objective of tourists now coming to the islands.

On the lip of Haleakala, at an altitude of 10,000 feet, there is a new concrete rest house, making it possible for one to remain at the crater as long as desired.

Other points of interest on Maui are:

IAO VALLEY—"The Yosemite of Hawaii." Half-hour motor drive from Wailuku. Easy and delightful trip.

PUUNENE SUGAR MILL.—Largest of its kind in the world. Located 2½ miles from Kahului. Area of plantation, 20,000 acres.

HAIKU PINEAPPLE DISTRICT.—From 5 to 7 miles from Paia. Homesteading center with pineapple cannery.

LAHAINA.—Oldest white settlement on island and first capital of group. Formerly great rendezvous of whaling fleets during winter months. Game-fishing; boats and tackle always accessible.

KEANAE VALLEY.—A large and fertile valley on windward side of East Maui. A few remaining glimpses of near primitive Hawaiian life may yet be found there.

KAUIKI HEAD (Hana).—A crater promontory at entrance of harbor, of historic interest. Noted stronghold of a Maui king during conquest of Kamehameha, which withstood siege of two years. Fine harbor connects with Ditch Trail.

WAILUKU.—County seat, theatres, courthouse, armory. Tourist headquarters. Four miles from Kahului.

KAHULUI.—Principal seaport with breakwater, windward Maui.

Make Arrangements for Your Trip to Maui With Mr. Newton, Information Bureau, Young Hotel Lobby

Maui Hotel promotional brochure, circa 1916-1922.

Hawaiian Airlines inter-island airplane, 1940s. Hawaiian Airlines first flew to Maui in 1941, after its name change from Inter-Island Airways.

Grand Hotel luggage sticker, 1930s or 1940s.

Grand Hotel, Wailuku, 1940s, Maui's most luxurious.

NOTABLE VISITORS

Amongst Maui's famous visitors, Herman Melville remains unique - he was on the lam. In 1843, before gaining fame as the author of *Moby Dick*, Melville jumped ship in the Marquesas, hopped a whaler and landed in Lahaina.

Mark Twain, on the other hand, arrived with a more legitimate pursuit - to write accounts of his travels for the *Sacramento Bee*. Although he planned to stay for six days in 1866, Maui's charms kept him five weeks. Twain's enchantment was so consuming that he never put pen to paper, claiming the visit "a perfect jubilee for me in the way of pleasure." One of his joys, a trip to the summit of Haleakalā, he later described in this way, "It was the sublimest spectacle I ever witnessed and I think the memory of it will remain with me always." He admired ʻĪao Valley so much that he used ʻĪao as the setting for a piece titled "Platonic Sweetheart." Upon leaving Maui, he admitted he had never "bade any place good-bye so regretfully."

Mark Twain's enthusiasm equalled that of fellow writer Jack London. In 1907, London and his wife Charmian became intrigued by Haleakalā, which they had viewed when approaching the island on their ship, the *Snark*. They were not disappointed. Haleakalā Ranch manager Louis von Tempsky led their party up the mountain, through the crater, and out Kaupō

Gap, followed by a two-day ride through the East Maui ditch country on a narrow, slippery trail bordering dramatic cliffs, numerous waterfalls and lush vegetation. London afterward touted this trip as the most satisfying that he had taken anywhere in the world. On a return trip in 1915, London joined Maui friends once again on the slopes of Haleakalā.

During the 1930s, a microcosm of American luminaries sought Maui's attractions. Representing Hollywood, Cecil B. DeMille evaluated Maui as a film production site, and Mary Pickford and Buddy Rogers honeymooned. Onlookers were delighted when humorist Will Rogers scored three goals at a polo match in Pukalani and when crooner Bing Crosby sang for the crowd at his steamer departure. Quite a few residents met the feisty George S. Patton during periodic visits to socialize and to challenge Maui's daring polo players. Artist Georgia O'Keeffe, alone amongst

these celebrities, left an enduring legacy. Her seven Hāna coast and ʻĪao Valley scenes exist as the only landscapes she ever produced of Hawaiʻi.

Betty Hutton, Ray Bolger, Joe E. Brown, Artie Shaw, Jack Carson, and Ray Anthony, as well as professional athletes such as Phil Rizzuto and Pee Wee Reese, just to mention a few, amused the multitude of military present on the island in World War II. Not surprisingly, perennial comic Bob Hope did his part, entertaining nearly 13,000 soldiers at a U.S.O. show at Paukūkalo in 1945.

After the war, the Hotel Hāna Maui became the island hot spot for celebrities such as Edward G. Robinson, Cornel Wilde, Joan Fontaine, Irving Berlin, and Samuel Goldwyn. To the present day, the luxuriousness of the island and its accommodations, combined with the warmth of its climate and its people, continue to attract leaders in government, industry, the arts, and entertainment.

The Jack London party at Hāna store, 1907. Charmian London is in the rear and Louis von Tempsky to the left. Jack himself was perhaps the photographer as he is not in view.

Mark Twain, a visitor to Maui in 1866. Although Twain praised Maui throughout his life, he never returned.

Georgia O'Keeffe during her visit to Hawai'i, 1939.

Frank Sinatra in Lahaina, 1960. Lahaina was converted to a Tahitian port town for the filming of The Devil at Four O'Clock.

MAUI COUNTY FAIR

Come one, come all to the Maui County Fair! It delights and diverts, enthralls and engrosses, transports and transfixes! Everyone knows that when it comes to fairs, Maui is truly nō ka 'oi - the best! The excitement of the Maui County Fair has unfolded each October since 1916 for faithful fairgoers, disappointing its fans only in 1917, 1918 and from 1942 to 1946.

The inaugural Maui County Fair, held at Wells Park in Wailuku, reflected Hawai'i's magnetic mix of Polynesia, Asia and rural America by offering arts and crafts, agricultural and livestock exhibits, a Japanese lantern procession, Hawaiiana, international dancing, band music, and a kickoff parade consisting of thousands of wide-eyed children. Once in the fairgrounds, the parading children rushed en masse to marvel at Daisy the elephant, undoubtedly the star attraction.

Maui demanded more of the same! Although the site of subsequent fairs shifted to Kahului, the roster of events so successful at the first fair remained, supplemented by E. K. Fernandez Joy Zone amusement rides, sideshows, baby and beauty contests, fireworks, photography, dog shows, auto displays, harmonica competitions and bullfrog jumping challenges.

Fair organizers lured a wide world of enjoyment and adventure to the remote island. Singers, dancers, acrobats and magicians alternated with circus acts accompanied by exotic animals. Real-live American Indians, unsteady in their moccasins from their first sea voyage, roused the curiosity of 1934 Wild West Show audiences. Four years later, a gala Ice Follies performed on the first ice rink in Hawai'i. Afterwards the slippery surface hosted a sea of fairgoers more adept astride breaking waves than blades, who weaved, wobbled and sprawled over the ice.

A Maui County Fair without sports was unimaginable. A program of over 25 sports - boxing, tennis, golf, yacht racing, soap box derby, jujitsu, and baseball, to name a few - often attracted both amateur and professional athletes from other islands and the mainland. The sports for which the Maui County Fair was most noted, however, were horseracing, which attracted the finest horses in the territory, and traditional football games between high school rivals.

The Maui County Fair was the undisputed highlight of Maui's year. Businesses shut down, children took a day off from school, and everyone headed to the Kahului fairgrounds. Residents saved their money throughout the year, many taking advantage of the Maui County Fair Savings Club offered by employers. Mauians walked, rode horses, drove, caught the Kahului Railroad, or packed into trucks provided by the plantations, and somehow they made it to the Fair. In 1947, when Maui had a population of 43,000, the attendance at the fair hit 60,000.

Maui residents were not the only enthusiasts. The Maui County Fair, advertised not only territory-wide but also nationally, enticed crowds that booked inter-island steamers to capacity at fair time. The Honolulu newspapers spiritedly promoted the event, recognizing its preeminence in island entertainment.

The 1931 Maui County Fair slogan, "Pau Hana Hana, Go Holo Holo!" or "Finish Work, Go Out for Pleasure!", fell on eager ears, for the refrain of an old song that slipped easily into local lyrics echoed Mauians' perpetual desire, "Take me to Kahului, Louie. Take me to the fair!"

Children enjoying Maui's first fair, held at Wells Park, Wailuku, 1916.

The fairground from the air, 1930s.

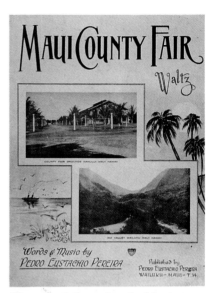

Sheet music honoring the Maui County Fair, 1929.

The star attraction at the 1916 Maui County Fair, Daisy the elephant.

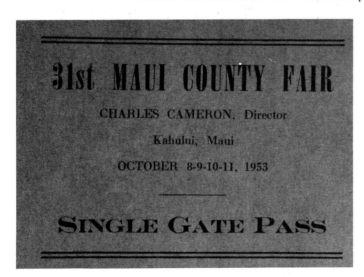

Lawrence "Chu" Baldwin and Lorna von Tempsky at racegrounds, 1920s.

The Royal Hawaiian Band performing at the first Maui County Fair, 1916.

Maui's very first Maui County Fair parade, 1916.

TALENTED ISLANDERS

Three unique individuals, different from each other in so many ways, had one thing in common - talent. History honors these Mauians in the arts - one a well-known actress, another a best-selling author, and the last a world-famous musician.

Exotic Polynesia, with its swaying palms, moonlit beaches and undulating hula dancers, provided a popular and romantic backdrop for movies in the early years of the industry, but choice parts depicting islanders almost always went to non-Polynesians. Part-Hawaiian actress Mamo Clark, a resident of Kīhei, became a notable exception to this practice. In California to study law, she took a screen test that catapulted her into the enviable position of playing opposite Clark Gable in the 1935 production of *Mutiny on the Bounty*. The beautiful, long-haired actress portrayed the Tahitian chiefess Maimiti, who wins the heart of Christian Fletcher. After playing roles in movies such as *Hurricane* and *Hawai'i Calls*, she once again encountered rebellion on the high seas as a character in *Mutiny on the Blackhawk*.

Hollywood also came calling on a local author named Armine von Tempsky. Her first novel, a romance titled *Hula* published in 1927, almost immediately appeared on the movie screens across America as a Paramount Pictures silent film starring Clara Bow. Von Tempsky subsequently wrote screenplays for both Metro Goldwyn Mayer and Grand National, as well as short stories and novels.

Seven of von Tempsky's 12 novels were set on Maui, specifically *Hula, Hawaiian Harvest, Bright Spurs, Pam's Paradise Ranch, Ripe Breadfruit, Aloha*, and her best-known work, *Born in Paradise*. *Born in Paradise*, a Literary Guild selection, and its sequel, *Aloha*, colorfully and affectionately portray her idyllic childhood on Haleakalā Ranch. The opening of *Born in Paradise* reflects the recurrent theme of von Tempsky's writing, "Attaining Paradise in the hereafter does not concern me greatly. I was born in Paradise."

Another child of Maui deserves recognition as one of the world's finest operatic tenors. Known as Hawai'i's Caruso, Hāna-born-and-raised Tandy MacKenzie unquestionably merits acclaim as the most famous native Hawaiian singer of all time. Discovered while attending school on the mainland, patrons encouraged him to develop his voice for opera, which he subsequently did through study in the United States, Canada and Europe.

Henry Ford heard MacKenzie perform during an early stage of his career and enticed him to Detroit, where Ford paid him to sing to his workers during daily recreation hours, thus financing MacKenzie's musical education. Audiences attending his concerts throughout the world in the 1920s and 1930s deluged him with applause. After a performance in Munich, fervent fans forced MacKenzie to return for 31 curtain calls and then hoisted him on their shoulders for a triumphant journey from the opera house to his hotel.

Reviewers gushed. What a voice! Exquisite! Glorious and complete! Rich and gorgeous in color! Such unusual beauty and purity! Bravos from opera aficionados around the world led to a recording contract with Columbia and parts in four Hollywood movies.

Although his first love was opera, MacKenzie never abandoned his musical heritage and would include Hawaiian songs in his concert repertoire, thereby introducing Hawaiian music to a worldwide audience. In 1922, and again in 1927, he returned home to Maui and provided several concerts to enthralled local audiences. Emotions soared to their highest when MacKenzie powerfully voiced his final song and sincere wish, "Aloha 'Oe." *The Maui News* reported that Maui "paid tribute to her son, heartily and with a feeling of mingled joy and reverence."

The three pioneering talents of Clark, von Tempsky and MacKenzie founded an island tradition which is flourishing today, as Maui continues as a creative center for writers, musicians and actors.

Mamo Clark in her best known role as the Tahitian chiefess Maimiti, playing opposite Clark Gable in Mutiny on the Bounty, *1935.*

Second from left, Armine von Tempsky, with her sisters, Lorna, Gwen, and Aina and brother Errol, 1920s.

A costumed Armine von Tempsky, 1920s, reflecting her spirited personality.

Tandy MacKenzie as Canio in I Pagliacci, *1930s.*

Mamo Clark in a publicity shot for the movie, Wallaby Jim of the Islands, *1937.*

FOCUS ON SPORTS

Maui was sports-crazy! Everyone participated by playing, coaching or as a spectator. Many managed to do all three, finding fun and excitement in an otherwise quiet community. While individual ethnic groups retained their traditional sports, such as Japanese sumo wrestling and a Filipino ball game called sipa, immigrant groups immediately adopted American sports, as well.

In 1908, only 13 years after the arrival of the first immigrants from Japan, organized Japanese baseball teams filled diamonds in Lahaina and Wailuku. Ethnicity, as well as locale, played a part in the formation of teams and leagues, with names such as the Pā'ia Portuguese, the Pu'unēnē Nippons, and the Filipino Plantation League. Athletic associations abounded in each community, however small.

Athletes on O'ahu, not limiting themselves to established rules, invented island-style barefoot football, a highly popular sport on Maui from the 1920s through the 1940s. Playing the game with no shoes, a natural outgrowth of the local habit of going shoeless, reduced the cost of participating. Enthusiastic fans watched talented toes punt the ball up to 80 yards.

Golf mania hit Maui early. The first links in Kahului opened in 1912, followed shortly by the construction of small courses throughout the island. Even Makawao School had its own course in the

1920s. The territory boasted its first municipal golf course when Waiehu opened in 1930.

Emphasis on sports developed many Maui champions, far more than history would expect from such a small island. Each decade showcased at least one star athlete. Tony do Rego played catcher for the Saint Louis Browns in the 1920s, followed by wrestler Oki (Jack) Shikina, who ascended to the level of contender for the world's heavyweight title. Wally Yonamine competed as a backfield ace for the San Francisco Forty-Niners in the late 1940s at the same time Emerick Ishikawa was winning consecutive national weightlifting championships. Shortly thereafter, Olowalu-born boxer Dado Marino battled his way to the title of 1950 flyweight champion of the world, and Ralph Yoshida triumphed nationally in his lightweight weightlifting class. Happy Valley boy and sumo pioneer Jesse Kuhaulua, known professionally as Takamiyama, rose to prominence in the 1960s, reaching a pinnacle in 1972 as the first non-Japanese to win the Emperor's Cup, Japan's most prestigious championship.

More than any island athletes, however, Maui's swimmers truly made waves. Olympic star and short-term Maui resident Clarence Crabbe, better known as Buster, represented the island in swim meets in the early 1920s. The arrival of the golden era of swimming on Maui, however, awaited the leadership of a Pu'unēnē School teacher named

Soichi Sakamoto.

Sakamoto started coaching with no training of his own and no pool for his athletes to swim in. As a result, swimmers had to use an eight-foot wide and three-foot deep Pu'unēnē irrigation ditch as an improvised raceway, building strength and endurance by struggling against the natural flow of the ditch water. Recognizing the need for proper facilities, the Hawaiian Commercial & Sugar Company built a pool, enabling Sakamoto to progress with his vision of athletic prominence.

In 1937, Sakamoto convinced 120 Pu'unēnē youngsters, aged 9 to 14, to join the Three Year Swim Club, an organization focused on a lofty ambition - competing at the Helsinki Olympics scheduled three years later. To reach this goal, members committed themselves to practice every day, including Sundays and holidays. Coach Sakamoto himself labored at the pool every day from 2:30 until midnight on school days, and from 6:00 a.m. until midnight otherwise. Within the year, a club member named Kiyoshi (Keo) Nakama stunned the Hawaiian swimming community by defeating an Olympic champion in a Honolulu meet.

Maui proceeded to dominate the territorial swimming scene, going on to even greater heights representing Hawai'i at mainland meets. In 1938, Nakama and Takashi Hirose placed in four events at the United States Amateur Athletic Union Championship. In the following year, a team composed of Nakama,

Hirose, Jose Balmores, Bill Neunzig, and Benny Castro triumphed as the overall men's AAU national champs. Due to their remarkable records, Nakama and Hirose earned places on the All-American Swim Team and repeated their swimming success internationally.

It seemed nothing could stop the Maui athletes. But something did. The Three Year Swim Club dream tragically sank when the Olympic Committee cancelled the 1940 games due to the war in Europe.

The Maui swimmers maintained their phenomenal momentum by winning overall honors in both the 1940 and 1941 AAU Nationals, compiling three consecutive years as the nation's top men's swim team! Maui's young female stars shared the spotlight. Thirteen-year-old Fujiko Katsutani captured the 200-meter breaststroke championship, first in 1939 and again in 1940. Following close behind her, Chieko Miyamoto tasted victory in the 300-meter individual medley in 1940, a feat she duplicated in 1941. Their successes in 1940 led the women's team to a fourth-place finish.

In 1940, Honolulu resident Bill Smith moved to Maui to benefit from Sakamoto's coaching and, within a year, broke several world records. He went on to win several AAU titles, compete with the All-American Swim Team, and win runner-up honors for the Sullivan Trophy as the outstanding amateur athlete in America three years in a row. Smith, along with other Maui swimmers, continued to garner honors throughout the war era in AAU, military and collegiate competitions. Shortly after the war, Sakamoto accepted a position as the University of Hawai'i swim coach.

By the time the Olympics were resumed after World War II, the members of the Three Year Swim Club were past their prime. Only latecomer Bill Smith qualified for the 1948 Olympic team slated for England. Fortunately, however, Smith realized Coach Sakamoto's dream by winning two gold medals in the 400-meter freestyle and as a member of the 800-meter freestyle relay, both in record time.

Swimming's highest recognition went to Buster Crabbe in 1965, when he was selected as a charter member of the International Swimming Hall of Fame. Just one year later, Soichi Sakamoto and Bill Smith joined the same prestigious honor roll. To this day, the Keo Nakama Outdoor Meet, held in Honolulu every year since 1946, pays homage to Keo Nakama, Sakamoto's first national champion.

Hopefully, young athletes on Maui will remember the discipline and dogged perseverance of the champions that have preceded them, particularly those Three Year Swim Club members of long ago, forced by necessity to train in the muddy waters of an irrigation ditch.

A sumo match at Pu'unene, 1920s.

Japanese baseball team, central Maui, 1930s.

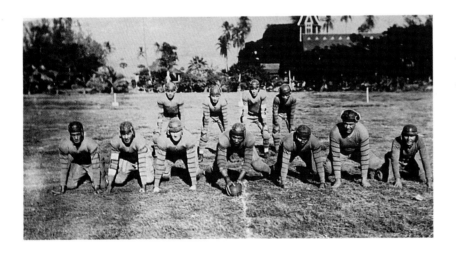

Lahaina Town football team, early 1920s. The first football teams on Maui competed in Wailuku in 1902.

Coach Y. B. Chur, on left, and his Maui Pineapple Company Recreation Center basketball team, 1940 winners of the Four Island Amateur Athletic Federation championship.

Coach Soichi Sakamoto and his team that won the AAU national outdoor championship in Santa Barbara, California, 1940.

The Puʻunēnē swimming tank, the training site for Maui's world-class swimmers.

The first West Maui golf course, mid-1930s. The greens had to be fenced to keep out free-ranging cattle. In case a ball hit a cow on the fairway; the golfer got another shot - no penalty!

HORSERACING AND POLO - ISLAND TRADITIONS

A Hawaiian prophet once declared, "White people shall come here. They shall bring dogs with very long ears, and men shall ride upon them." This prediction came true in 1803, when King Kamehameha I became the first Hawaiian to sit astride a horse, one of three delivered to him in Lahaina by Captain Richard J. Cleveland of the HMS *Lelia Byrd*.

Although Kamehameha was initially unimpressed, interest in horses rapidly grew throughout the island. Over the years, Maui developed a tradition of fine horsemanship, not only for practical purposes, but also for the excitement generated by the fast-paced sports of horseracing and polo.

Maui's first race track, built around the 1850s at Lahaina, remained popular with West Maui horse fans until the latter 1920s. It was at a track in Kahului, however, where Maui earned its stellar reputation.

The newly formed Maui Racing Association organized its first racing schedule at Kahului in 1886. Their premiere meet, held on the Fourth of July each year, attracted the fastest horses from all parts of the territory. In the early days, various communities on Maui showed their support by offering prizes, such as a Waihe'e purse or a Kula purse, and individuals provided rewards, as well.

Queen Lili'uokalani was one of these donors, for the quality of racing traditionally attracted the interest, and sometimes the presence, of Hawaiian royalty. Everybody went to the races! Men, women, and children of all ethnic backgrounds spiritedly cheered on their favorites. Mauians and their off-island guests enjoyed not only horseracing, but also various forms of entertainment, often Hawaiian music or a fancy dress ball, offered during this celebrated social season.

Hawaiian-style racing at Kahului was anything but dull. Jockeys of every ethnic background rode horses colorfully named 'Āina Nui, Pi'iholo or Hāmākuapoko Boy. Competition included distinctive events such as the Oriental Race, in which the horse had to be owned and ridden by an Asian; the Manager's Race, which pitted plantation managers against each other; and several types of races for cowboys from Maui's many ranches. Occasionally a mule race added even more spice to the program.

In 1917, the Maui Racing Association integrated with the newly formed Maui County Fair and Racing Association, thereby donating its Kahului site for the fair. As a result, fair-time horseracing got its start at the second Maui County Fair of 1919, and thereafter reigned as the blue ribbon event of the territorial racing season. Thousands of fervent fans came from throughout the islands to watch the action from crowded grandstands.

Maui horse owners also entered other races on the Fourth of July and Kamehameha Day, as well as those off-island. Maui merited a first-rate reputation, for, wherever horses ran, Valley Islanders frequented the winner's circle. Horseracing's heyday ceased abruptly in 1941, due to the pressures of war. Although revived afterward, and continued off and on into the 1970s, Maui's enthusiasm for the sport of kings never reached its former level.

The birth of polo on Maui followed closely on the hooves of horseracing. Louis von Tempsky, considered the "Father of Hawaiian Polo," formed the initial Maui polo team in 1887 with daring men willing to play reckless and primitive games on barely-trained mounts. It was said that the players rode anything with four legs, which at times included mules and colts, as well as horses. Not surprisingly, battles between horse and rider, bucking incidents, and runaways down the field disrupted matches with annoying regularity. These first games utilized a Makawao pasture owned by George Miner, now the site of the Makawao Hongwanji Mission.

The polo schedule grew more regular after the founding of the Makawao Polo Club in 1899. In order to accommodate a growing number of spectators, the action moved to more centrally located Sunnyside, between Pā'ia and Makawao. The following year O'ahu awakened to polo when a few young men, having spent their summer vacations on Maui, returned to their home island as eager players. What was to develop into a long-standing rivalry originated in 1901 when Oʻahu defeated Maui in the first inter-island game.

Polo continued to expand throughout Hawaiʻi, with the Black and Gold Maui team frequently capturing inter-island championships. Maui's success, however, was not limited to the Territory of Hawaiʻi, for Maui players and ponies gained attention in mainland play. In 1913, the All-American polo team asked to borrow William Baldwin's horse, Carry the News, and, with the superbly trained mount's assistance, emerged victorious in international competition. As a result, many considered Carry the News to be the most famous polo pony in the world.

The sport of polo suffered a shocking tragedy in 1925, when 14 of the finest Maui mounts perished in a stable fire at the Maui Polo Grounds in Pukalani. Not hindered for long, owners trained new ponies and competition resumed.

Polo great Frank F. Baldwin gained wide recognition in a career highlighted by membership on the All-American team of 1913. Matching Frank's accomplishments, his son Edward Baldwin led the Black and Gold to its greatest glory in the 1930s. Other nationally ranked players such as Samuel Baldwin, David T. Fleming, Harold W. Rice, Lawrence "Chu" Baldwin, Asa Baldwin, Richard "Manduke" Baldwin, and Harold F. "Oskie" Rice made Maui teams a powerhouse on the field. From 1916 until World War II, these outstanding players hosted their rivals at the Maui Polo

Grounds located between Pukalani and Hāliʻimaile, commonly called the Pukalani polo field.

Oʻahu Army team captain George S. Patton coined the nickname "Maui Cowboys" for the Black and Gold team that led him to defeat in 1935. Although not intended as a compliment, the nickname was apt, as the Maui players spent much of their time in the saddle overseeing their vast ranches and, therefore, played a rough-and-tumble game. Maui's success in inter-isle play inspired other nicknames such as the Golden Wave, and even the Golden Typhoon.

Polo attracted a cross-section of Maui residents. When the matches were at Sunnyside, polo fans travelled via special trains to and from Wailuku. Major competitions at the Pukalani field attracted thousands of spectators from all walks of life. No admission was charged and everyone was welcome. As a consequence, polo symbolized sportsman-

ship on the Valley Island. When Maui's team was on the field, the players knew they had the support of the entire community.

Polo was put on hold during World War II, and during that time the military transformed the field's green expanse into a huge quartermaster and infantry depot. Fortunately, isle enthusiasts revived the sport in 1950 at its current indoor arena site above Pukalani, and later in the 1970s at an Olinda outdoor arena. Today Mauians can enjoy a Sunday morning on the slopes of Haleakalā watching sleek horses and dashing players compete as aggressively as the famed Black and Gold. As in yesteryear, Maui commands respect in both national and international play. Polo has come a long way since that long-gone era when Maui's first players, mounted on bucking mules, spent half their time retrieving wild shots from neighboring guava bushes.

The stables at the Pukalani polo field, 1920s.

Polo teams in action at the Pukalani field, 1920s.

Left to right, Mrs. Ervin, Louise Dillingham, Ruth Baldwin, Alice Castle and Jane Hunt, polo spectators at game in California, 1929.

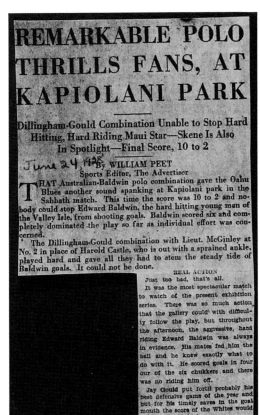

REMARKABLE POLO THRILLS FANS, AT KAPIOLANI PARK

Dillingham-Gould Combination Unable to Stop Hard Hitting, Hard Riding Maui Star—Skene Is Also In Spotlight—Final Score, 10 to 2

June 24, 1928

By WILLIAM PEET
Sports Editor, The Advertiser

THAT Australian-Baldwin polo combination gave the Oahu Blues another sound spanking at Kapiolani park in the Sabbath match. This time the score was 10 to 2 and nobody could stop Edward Baldwin, the hard hitting young man of the Valley Isle, from shooting goals. Baldwin scored six and completely dominated the play so far as individual effort was concerned.

The Dillingham-Gould combination with Lieut. McGinley at No. 2 in place of Harold Castle, who is out with a sprained ankle, played hard and gave all they had to stem the steady tide of Baldwin goals. It could not be done.

REAL ACTION

Just too bad, that's all.

It was the most spectacular match to watch of the present exhibition series. There was so much action that the gallery could with difficulty follow the play, but throughout the afternoon, the aggressive, hard riding Edward Baldwin was always in evidence. His mates fed him the ball and he knew exactly what to do with it. He scored goals in four our of the six chukkers and there was no riding him off.

Jay Gould put forth probably his best defensive game of the year and but for his timely saves in the goal mouth the score of the Whites would have mounted higher.

Paired with Baldwin and a potent point getter for his team was Skene, the Englishman, who also played a whale of a game.

Honolulu Advertiser article, June 24, 1928.

Maui players on the field, San Mateo, California, 1929.

Maui's team, late 1920s. Second from left, Frank Baldwin, and sons, left to right, Edward, Lawrence "Chu" and Asa.

Local jockey Harold Amoral riding Kapalaea, 1939.

Horseracing at Kahului, late 1930s, with jockeys Clarence Sakamoto and Adam Jardine.

LAHAINA

Ancient chiefs, like visitors of today, looked with favor upon Lahaina. They basked in its dry, balmy weather and mountain-to-sea beauty, while taking advantage of its strategic position close to Lāna'i and Moloka'i. The West Maui Mountains provided ample water for taro cultivation from Olowalu to Honokōhau, and the sea generously supplied them fish. Nature's abundance sustained not only chiefs and their extensive retinues, but also the largest population on Maui.

As a population center and site of chiefly power, the Lahaina district endured many bloody battles, often over Maui sovereignty. One particular battle between Peleioholani of O'ahu and Alapa'inui of the island of Hawai'i in 1783 gained notoriety for its ferociousness - to this day, bones from the slaughter remain scattered under the ground all the way from Lahaina to Honokōwai. During his 1795 campaign of conquest, the famed Kamehameha himself plundered Lahaina. Apparently finding Lahaina to his liking, he returned seven years later for an extended stay to prepare for the conquest of Kaua'i, his final effort to secure a united Hawaiian kingdom. During this time he constructed what was called a two-story brick "palace," the first western-style house in the kingdom.

As an easily accessible port, Lahaina was one of the first settlements on Maui to be described by Westerners. A 1793 visitor declared Lahaina "...neatly divided into little fields and laid out in the highest state of cultivation and improvement...", while another observer 25 years later claimed, "The environs of Lahaina are like a garden."

Kauikeaouli, King Kamehameha III, made Lahaina his home from the 1820s through the 1840s. As a consequence, during that time Lahaina served as the capital of the kingdom and the site where Hawai'i's first constitution was written. Kauikeaouli preferred the free life of Lahaina over Honolulu, illustrated by this episode recorded by a foreign resident, "...I heard some voices chanting a Hawaiian oli-oli, and perceived as the party drew near, the king and queen [and others] linked arm in arm, marching up the street in a most jolly way, singing. The rain was warm, the air soft, and the company needed but the scantiest clothing - no shoes or stockings, but with sweet smelling maile wreaths for dress suits..."

The independent-minded Kauikeaouli never converted to Christianity despite Lahaina's ever-present missionaries, but he did accept many of their nonreligious teachings. For that reason, Maui's first Protestant station, established at Lahaina in 1823, was undoubtedly one of Hawai'i's most significant. Through their access to Kauikeaouli, Lahaina missionaries molded the infant Hawaiian government, and, through the establishment of Lahainaluna High School, they shaped the lives of countless other Hawaiian leaders.

Starting in 1819, whaling lured thousands of sailors to Lahaina, where they enriched its coffers and tested the forbearance of its Christian missionaries. Sailors of the whaling fleet, seeking pleasures in the bottle and in the arms of women after years of whaling in northern waters, were not pleased when these diversions were denied them by a missionary-influenced ban. In two separate incidents, sailors attacked the mission residence. After the whaling ship *John Palmer* fired its cannon into the village, a fort was built for the protection of Lahaina's citizens. By the late 1830s, however, the prohibition no longer existed, and Lahaina lapsed once again into drunkenness and debauchery.

By the mid-1800s, Lahaina earned mixed reviews. A traveller approaching from afar praised Lahaina as "all fresh and lovely with sunshine and verdure...." But a closer view showed Lahaina to be full of fleas, mosquitoes, and dusty roads "obnoxious to pedestrians."

The dusty roads led to two churches (one for seamen and another for natives), a few schoolhouses, a seamen's hospital, a customhouse which doubled as a post office, and the brick palace. Various waterfront stores, warehouses and sheds catered to the inter-island shipping and whaling trades, while numerous grog shops and boarding houses pandered to its oftentimes rowdy residents. Not surprisingly, Lahaina required a jail. A census of Lahaina in 1846 enumerated 3,445 Hawaiians and 112 foreigners (not counting whalers) living in nearly 1,100 structures, most composed of grass and adobe.

With the decline of the whaling trade in the 1860s, Lahaina turned to the emerging sugar industry to fill the economic void. Hawaiian scholar David Malo, one of the earliest to experiment with sugar in West Maui, grew cane in the 1840s in both Lahaina and Kāʻanapali. In the next decade, several small companies planted cane wherever land could be obtained. What was to become the Pioneer Mill Company set a fast pace. Within ten years of its founding in 1862, the company tasted sweet success as one of the largest operations in Hawaiʻi.

Visitors to Lahaina at the turn of the century saw a "charming, drowsy and dreamy village," connected to Wailuku by a several-hour trip over the one-lane Pali Road, nicknamed Amalfi Drive for its spectacularly scenic views evocative of Amalfi, Italy. The landmark Pioneer Hotel (now Inn), constructed in 1901, joined a few other small hostelries welcoming business travellers and the occasional tourist. Many years would pass before the numbers of visitors to Lahaina would outgrow these accommodations.

Lahaina's early churches included Waineʻe (now called Waiola), first established in 1823; Maria Lanakila, or Our Lady of Victory, built in 1858; and the Church of the Holy Innocents, an Episcopal Church dating from 1862. Several smaller Catholic and Protestant Churches served neighboring localities. The Chinese worshipped at the Wo Hing Society Clubhouse and Japanese immigrants met their spiritual needs through Buddhist temples founded in the plantation era.

Lahaina evolved into a plantation town as agriculture's economic importance increased. West Maui's first pineapple prospered at Honolua Ranch in 1912, the gold of pineapple eventually filling out the landscape along with sugar's green. The plantations employed the area's residents in field, cannery and mill. Workers lived free in company housing and, when they shopped at the plantation store or took in a movie at the Pioneer Theater, they paid for both through payroll deduction. The 1930 plantation economy supported a population of almost 7,000 in Lahaina proper, with 2,000 additional people spread from Olowalu to Honokōhau.

Independent businesses, many owned by Chinese and Japanese, flourished along Front Street. Unfortunately, a disastrous fire raged through the Lahaina business district in 1919, destroying many structures. Lahaina was hard hit once again when a 1946 tidal wave devastated homes and stores up and down the coast.

Despite these setbacks, much of old Lahaina town remains, its layers of history awaiting discovery, not only by professional archaeologists, but also by anyone with imagination. Consider the century-old Pioneer Inn. Those in the proper frame of mind can easily envision the land's occupation as an ancient and royal taro patch.

Front Street, Lahaina, 1940.

Pioneer Hotel, Lahaina, around 1910.

Pioneer Hotel, 1901, festooned with greenery marking its opening.

Front Street looking toward the present-day seawall in the aftermath of the disastrous Lahaina fire of 1919. The safe of the Lahaina branch of the Bank of Maui survives at left.

Māla Wharf, 1928.

Black Point Wharf, Kāʻanapali, 1920s.
(Right) View from the air.

Honokōhau Valley, before 1908.   In view is the first Honokohau Catholic
Church, located well up into the valley where once there was a sizeable
population.

Travelling on the Pali Road from Lahaina, 1880s.

Lumber unloaded into ocean in front of Lahaina Courthouse, receiving the benefit of a salt water cure, 1908.

Harvesting akule at Honolua Bay, around 1930s. Baldwin Packers maintained a boathouse there to house akule skiffs.

Lahaina at the turn of the century, with fish drying racks and sugar warehouse in foreground.

PĀ'IA

The town of Pā'ia was fabricated from water and sugar. In 1878, water from the newly completed Hāmākua Ditch turned large tracts of land at the Alexander and Baldwin Plantation in East Maui into fields of vigorous sugar cane. In order to process the resulting crops, the plantation built a mill at Pā'ia in 1880, thereby creating a community where little had existed before.

In 1903, the profitable sugar operation, by then renamed the Pā'ia Plantation, merged with its sister Ha'ikū Sugar Company to form the Maui Agricultural Company. Three years later the newly organized company built a larger, improved Pā'ia mill. From its inception until 1946, Harry A. Baldwin presided over Maui Agricultural Company. Baldwin was also president of several other firms, a member of the Territorial Senate for many years, and served as Hawai'i's delegate to Congress in 1922. On his death, the county dedicated a Pā'ia-area beach park in his memory.

Upper Pā'ia, site of the mill, burgeoned with plantation camps housing mill and field workers of every ethnic background. Several camps clustered around the mill, while others fanned out beyond Pā'ia. In the town's heyday in the 1930s and 1940s, most of Pā'ia's population of more than 10,000 lived in Upper Pā'ia, shopped at the Pā'ia Store and smaller outlying camp stores, frequented Nashiwa Bakery, and enjoyed movies and amateur contests at the Orpheum and Pā'ia theaters. The company-run Pā'ia Store was no small-time operation! Clerks throughout the rambling two-story building sold just about everything - groceries, hardware, dry goods, clothing, and furniture, while mechanics repaired ailing automobiles and soda jerks dispensed fountain refreshments to the thirsty.

In contrast to Upper Pā'ia, the plantation did not own the land of Lower Pā'ia. Private entrepreneurs served a primarily plantation clientele through a vast number of retail businesses - stores, meat and fish markets, restaurants and bars, service stations, barber shops, photo studios, and small Japanese hotels. Several theaters amused the populace over time, including the Lower Pā'ia and Princess theaters.

Pā'ia was a self-contained world. Its citizens enjoyed their own library and gym and sent their children to Pā'ia School, the largest on Maui. To entertain themselves, some cheered on barbed birds at cockfights, while others attended Japanese plays called shibais. Nearly all participated in a diversity of sports programs and attended one of several Buddhist, Shinto, Protestant, and Catholic churches in the area. Pā'ia Hospital, later used as Maui Children's Home, cared for the sick and injured.

A massive fire in 1930 destroyed 15 stores and several other structures in Lower Pā'ia, requiring a portion of the town to be rebuilt. Disaster struck again in 1946, when a tsunami heavily damaged the community. However devastating, the effects of these tragedies were relatively short-lived. On the other hand, the residential development of Kahului in the 1950s, which lured thousands of sugar workers away with the prospect of owning their own homes, had a long-lasting deleterious effect on Pā'ia's prosperity.

The Maui Agricultural Company merged with the Hawaiian Commercial & Sugar Company in 1948, under which name the Pā'ia mill still grinds cane. Although the retail buildings in Pā'ia remain, almost all are filled with businesses catering to tourists and newcomers, particularly the large numbers of windsurfers that permeate the community. The residential camps are gone, and only a few Pā'ia plantation-era stores, such as the Pā'ia Clothes Cleaners, and Nagata and Horiuchi stores, survive as reminders of Pā'ia as it once was, a large and bustling sugar town.

Exterior view of the company-owned Pāʻia Store, 1930s. This gigantic store was one of many that served the town's 10,000 residents.

Pāʻia School lunch token, 1915-1935, good for a five-cent lunch. The hole in the center allowed the token to be secured on a string around the neck.

Inside view of early Pāʻia Store, destroyed by fire in 1910.

Spreckelsville Mill at the completion of its construction, 1882.

The corner of Hāna Highway and Baldwin Avenue, Lower Pā'ia, circa 1920, showing some of Lower Pā'ia's numerous privately owned businesses.

Harry A. Baldwin, Maui Agricultural Company manager, with wife Ethel, 1922. At this time Baldwin was Hawai'i's delegate to Congress, having been elected upon the death of Prince Kūhiō.

Pā'ia railroad depot around 1910. Kahului Railroad transported both sugar and passengers to and from upper Pā'ia after tracks were laid in 1905.

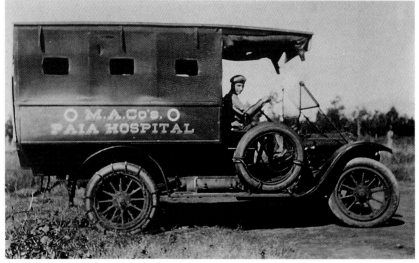

Possibly the first ambulance on isle, purchased for use at Maui Agricultural Company's Pā'ia Hospital in 1912. .

PUʻUNĒNĒ

At the turn of the century, the name Puʻunēnē designated only a volcanic cinder cone between Pāʻia and Spreckelsville, from whose height could be seen the surrounding plain. Sugar grower Henry P. Baldwin adopted Puʻunēnē, which means goose hill, for his nearby mill, inadvertently naming an entire community which was to grow up around it.

Nature designed the isthmus of Maui sparingly. An early traveller described it graphically, "a dreary expanse of sand and shifting sandhills... Trackless, glaring, choking, a guide is absolutely necessary to a stranger, for the footprints or wheel-marks of one moment are obliterated the next." The 1879 Spreckels irrigation ditch, followed by the 1882 Waiheʻe Ditch, and later ditches constructed by Hawaiian Commercial & Sugar Company, radically altered this barren landscape, turning a vast wasteland into a green carpet of sugar cane.

Hawaiian Commercial & Sugar Company's Puʻunēnē mill first processed cane in 1902, supplanting their previous smaller mill at Spreckelsville. At the time of its opening and for several years after, Puʻunēnē claimed the honor of being the largest sugar mill in the world. Four years after Puʻunēnē's first grind, Henry P. Balwin's son Frank followed his father in the leadership of the company, beginning a term of service that lasted for more than four decades.

The plantation itself was one of the world's largest, composed in 1935 of 33,000 acres, of which 16,000 was planted in cane. Twenty-six residential camps for employees sprawled over the plantation, stretching from Camp 1 in Spreckelsville near the northern coast to Camp 7 near Māʻalaea to the south. Many camps centered around Puʻunēnē itself, with colorful names such as Sam Sing, McGerrow and Spanish Camp echoing a multiracial work force.

More than 10,000 people lived and worked in this sugar town in 1930, making Puʻunēnē and its agricultural sister Pāʻia the two largest communities on Maui. The plantation provided a meat market, dairy, Camp 5 Store, a service station, and a hospital. In outlying camps, small privately owned stores not only sold groceries and other basic items, but also performed double-duty as social gathering places. Children filled the eight grades of Puʻunēnē School, and churches of all denominations dotted the community.

HC&S furnished a variety of recreational facilities for employees, including a swimming pool, bowling alley, tennis courts, ball fields, and clubhouses. Climaxing the plantation social season, a Harvest Home celebration marked the completion of the mill's grind each fall, drawing hundreds of participants from Maui, as well as off-island, to dance at an elaborate ball and to participate in sports tournaments.

In 1939, authorities chose the Puʻunēnē area as the site of Maui's primary airport. Just one year later, military needs triggered the airport's rapid expansion into the Puʻunēnē Naval Air Station. No longer needed after the war, the military abandoned the air station, and a few years later the island's general airport relocated to its present site in Kahului.

Puʻunēnē today whispers where before it boomed. While the mill still grinds its crop successfully, plantation employees have moved to Kahului and elsewhere, and cane grows where camps formerly thrived. And whatever happened to that cinder cone for which the town was named? In a way it still exists, though unseen, as it provided the base material for the Puʻunēnē road and airport.

Hawaiian Commercial & Sugar Company mill, with bowling alley on the right, 1915.

Pu'unēnē Clubhouse, 1915. Hawaiian Commercial & Sugar Company provided recreation, as well as housing and medical care, to their employees.

Pu'unēnē store around the turn of the century.

Puʻunēnē Avenue, early 1900s.

Hospital Camp, Puʻunēnē, 1930s. Twenty-six residential camps stretched over the 30,000-acre HC&S plantation.

KULA

Kula's ancient boundaries stretched all the way from mountain to ocean, far beyond what we consider Kula to be today. The name, meaning open country or plain (as opposed to valley or stream bottom), accurately characterized the dry district of Kula.

Hawaiians in the higher elevations of what we now identify as Kula traditionally grew sweet potatoes. This dietary staple was supplemented by poi brought in from the taro fields of Wailuku. Seeking to convert this populace, Protestant missionaries established a church at Kēōkea in 1840, coinciding with the region's rise to prominence in Irish potato cultivation.

Land suited so well to sweet potato cultivation was easily converted to growing white potatoes for the whaling trade. Whaling crews' tenacious loyalty to white potatoes influenced many a ship to land at Lahaina, rather than potato-poor Oʻahu. Kula's appearance in 1846 is described thus, "The crop now in the ground is immense. The fields being all in blossom have a fine appearance, spreading as they do over the broad surface of the mountain." Lumbering bullocks hauled a yearly crop of 20,000 barrels down the mountain to whaling ships anchored at Lahaina or Kalepolepo.

An even bigger boom was yet to come. The discovery of gold in California created a frantic demand for Kula's potatoes, onions and other vegetables, and prices shot to exorbitant levels. The population of Kula ballooned as enterprising individuals from throughout the kingdom, as well as immigrants direct from China, sought wealth in Kula soil.

A visitor familiar with conditions in both California and Kula claimed, "California is yonder in Kula. There is the gold without the fatigue and sickness of the mining country." Accordingly, Kula was nicknamed "Nu Kaleponi," meaning New California. California, however, soon became agriculturally self-sufficient, decimating the export trade in vegetables by the early 1850s.

Kula then returned to small-scale truck farming, producing corn, beans, onions, cabbage, wheat, cotton, and its traditional crop, sweet potatoes. Agricultural opportunities attracted a sizeable second wave of immigrant Chinese in the 1890s. Shortly thereafter, Portuguese settlers, lured by ranching, also migrated up the slopes of Haleakalā, followed later by Japanese who established farms and orchards.

Although intermittently plagued by drought, Kula prospered. Its hard-working residents purchased staples at several small Chinese stores, supplemented by the meat raised on Kula ranches and farms and fish brought from the coast. Opium smuggled through the port of Mākena made its way to Kula opium dens, where it could be had for 25 to 50 cents a smoke.

Public schools at Kēōkea and Waiakoa taught the ABCs to Kula's children, many of them Chinese who spoke only their native language. In addition, Chinese students attended one of three Chinese language schools for three hours a day, alongside a few Hawaiians.

Churches in Kula reflected the multiracial community. The Chinese attended either Saint John's Episcopal Church or the Waiakoa Church, while the Portuguese celebrated mass at either the octagonal Holy Ghost Church or Our Lady Queen of Angels. The Haleakalā Church at Kēōkea tended to a Hawaiian congregation. Many Chinese retained their original religion and worshipped at the Ket Hing Society clubhouse, which also served as a social and political gathering place.

A tragic increase in tuberculosis on Maui led civic leaders to choose Kula's cool climate and clean air for the site of what was eventually named the Kula Sanatorium. The Kula Sanatorium started on a shoestring budget in 1910 with its first patients housed in tents. More than once winds flattened the tents, distressing events which hastened the construction of wooden wards and cottages. In an effort to check tuberculosis before it started, a Preventorium opened in 1926, providing improved diet and health education to about 100 underweight children. Six years later, a newly constructed small general hospital cared for nontubercular patients on the sanatorium grounds.

The main 200-bed sanatorium building, designed by prominent architect Charles W. Dickey and paid for with federal Works Progress Administration funds, opened to acclaim in 1937. Tuberculosis experts touted Kula Sanatorium as one of the most modern and best-equipped tuberculosis facilities in the United States.

Kula San, as it was commonly called, achieved self-sufficiency through maintaining its own dairy, growing its own vegetables and fruit, and raising its own animals. Enforced isolation for stricken children necessitated a Kula Sanatorium grammar school. Fortunately, tuberculosis declined as a health threat in the 1950s, allowing Kula San to shift to other medical care services.

Increasing interest in Haleakalā as a tourist attraction in the mid-1950s inspired the construction of the Kula Lodge, followed a few years later by Hale Moi, later named the Silversword Inn. To this day, the Kula community's response to tourism has remained typically low-key.

Kula entered modern times gracefully, retaining its beauty, its agriculture and its distinctive charm. And its namesake onions, so popular with nineteenth-century California gold miners, are sweeter than ever!

Octagonal Holy Ghost Church, constructed by Portuguese immigrants in 1894.

Kula Sanatorium, 1920s.

A riding excursion at Ōmaʻopio, 1890s.

Kēōkea street scene, around 1940.

'ULUPALAKUA AND KAHIKINUI

Ancient Hawaiians flourished in a vastly different 'Ulupalakua and Kahikinui than we know today. More abundant rainfall sustained a larger forest zone of native trees, and the extensive cultivation of dryland taro and sweet potatoes, supplemented by coastal fishing, supported a sizeable Hawaiian population. Landscape and lifestyle alike began to crumble when free-ranging cattle, released in the 1790s, caused extensive damage to plant life, and when a foreign economy replaced the native system.

In the 1840s, Linton L. Torbert purchased a large piece of 'Ulupalakua for sugar cultivation, later growing potatoes for the California Gold Rush trade. In 1856, after a leaky ship ruined his potato shipments, Torbert faced bankruptcy, and the land was sold to former whaling captain and successful Honolulu businessman James Makee. Makee proceeded to plant cane, to import cattle, and to create what a visitor described as "an island of tranquil delight."

Makee planted 150,000 trees, mostly eucalyptus, thereby recasting the landscape with nonnative species. He built a New England-style mansion topped with a widow's walk, imported peacocks to stroll the grounds, and maintained a billiard room, a tennis court, and a bowling green for frequent visitors. His special guest and close friend, King Kalākaua, enjoyed his own cottage.

Roses, flowers rarely seen in the tropics, grew in abundance throughout the formal gardens of the Makee estate. Roses even lined the roadsides. This unusual botanical array inspired Makee to name his heavenly retreat the Rose Ranch. The spectacular roses were so famous, that a deep pink variety called lokelani was chosen as the official flower of the island of Maui and pink as its official color.

Although the plantation ranked as one of the largest sugar estates in the islands at its peak in the 1860s, a blight doomed cane production. As a consequence, the land was converted to ranch use exclusively in 1883. 'Ulupalakua Ranch, as it was subsequently known, became Maui's largest ranch through the acquisition of others in the area, notably the Kahikinui and Raymond ranches.

'Ulupalakua Ranch's reputation spread throughout the territory, because of its top-notch crew of skilled ranch hands headed by world champion roper Ikua Purdy. The cowboys' stature, along with that of other island paniolos, made Maui and the ranch a fitting location for the first Hawaiian rodeo championships in 1939.

More than just cattle and cowboys filled the vista at 'Ulupalakua, however. During the early 1930s, vast fields of potatoes yielded bumper crops, and the ranch leased 30-acre parcels of land rent-free to encourage diverse agriculture. With a population of 422 in 1930, the 'Ulupalakua community supported its own school, post office, stores and even its own courthouse. Later, a movie theater opened. Churchgoers spent their Sunday mornings at either of two long-established Protestant Hawaiian churches at 'Ulupalakua and Kanaio, or at St. James Catholic Church.

In many ways 'Ulupalakua is still an "island of tranquil delight." Although Makee's magnificent home and Kalākaua's cottage burned down in 1977, cattle remain a familiar sight in the picture-perfect countryside. A picturesque winery now complements the landscape, and the ranch grounds continue to beckon with the hospitality of a bygone era.

Kahikinui Ranch corral, 1920s.

(Both photos at top) ʻUlupalakua Ranch corral, 1927.

Kahikinui cowboys at work, 1927.

Edward Baldwin and family in front of ʻUlupalakua Ranch home, 1928.

MAKAWAO AND PUKALANI

In ancient times, unlike today, few made the Makawao or Pukalani area their home. But Hawaiians did utilize the region. The most significant remnant of Hawaiian presence in the area, a sacred hill called Puʻu Pane, rests largely unnoticed two miles above Pukalani. In days of old, Puʻu Pane supported a heiau, or temple for high chiefs, one of several known to have existed between Pukalani and Ōmaʻopio.

According to Hawaiian practice, all lands belonged to the aliʻi, or chiefs. Finding this idea alien and unprofitable, Westerners pushed for reform. Bowing to pressure in 1845, King Kamehameha III chose Makawao to announce an experiment whereby commoners could own land. Kamehameha III decreed that Hawaiians could purchase property throughout the district for one dollar an acre. As a consequence, nearly 100 parcels totalling over 900 acres sold. This first break in the feudal land system led three years later to the Great Mahele, a government policy which established a private system of land ownership throughout the kingdom.

In his milestone proclamation, Kamehameha III exempted only one piece of property from sale, a sugar plantation operated by William A. McLane. McLane's tract was the first of several early sugar endeavors in the Makawao area, notably the Hāliʻimaile Plantation, established in 1848. When the Hāliʻimaile Plantation was sold to Charles Brewer II, it became known as Brewer Plantation and then the Union Plantation, and Grove Ranch. In 1857, H. A. Spencer founded yet another pioneering upcountry sugar venture named the East Maui Plantation, or, as it was also known, the Kaluanui Plantation.

Starting in the 1870s, Tong Akana owned and operated the 12,500-acre Piʻiholo Plantation, now part of Haleakalā Ranch. Up until 1950, a 100-foot stone smokestack stood below Makawao as a reminder of this early enterprise. Ironically, this most visible remnant of several mills in the area never experienced the heat or ash generated by a productive operation, as its essential processing equipment was lost at sea.

Undoubtedly the most significant upcountry sugar operation began in 1969, when Henry P. Baldwin and Samuel T. Alexander purchased a 12-acre Hawaiian homestead for $110. They then enlarged their holdings by paying $8,000 for the 559-acre Bush Ranch located in an area known as Sunnyside, in lower Makawao. These seminal parcels became the foundation for the giant Alexander & Baldwin Corporation.

Makawao's expansive lands and ample rains supported more than sugar. Wheat-growing in Hawaiʻi, an almost exclusively Maui endeavor, centered in Makawao, not only due to favorable growing conditions, but also because of enthusiastic promotion by Reverend Jonathan S. Green. Wheat crops, small since the mid-1830s, increased exponentially in the 1850s as much-needed provisions for California gold rushers. In 1862, after demand from California declined, production totalled 25,000 bushels. A few years later wheat exports further dwindled and finally ceased.

The name Makawao, or edge of the forest, aptly characterizes its environs, for the area east of Makawao teemed with native ʻōhiʻa, kou, hau, māmane and koa trees. The commercial importance of richly hued koa wood attracted Maui's first water-powered sawmill, constructed in 1860 at Kaupakulua. A steam-propelled successor built in 1880 at Kaʻiliʻili above Kokomo also focused on koa, providing wood to both local and mainland markets. Nearly 7,000 feet of prime koa from this mill comprised the interior woodwork for King Kalākaua's opulent ʻIolani Palace, completed in 1882. The lumber business proved so profitable that by the turn of the century the koa forest was gone.

A visitor in the latter part of the nineteenth century described Makawao in this way, "Several stores, some kept by Chinese as butcher shops, and a couple of coffee-saloons and the post-office made up a tidy little township." Tidy in the sense of orderly, perhaps, but not clean. Residents attempting to travel from one place to another, however short a distance, became covered by either dust or mud. An immense cloud of powdery red earth encircling travellers from central Maui could be seen from long distances, giving warning of their arrival.

Hawaiians and Chinese first populated the town on the cool slopes of Haleakalā, followed by the Portuguese and Japanese, many cultivating their own plots or working on surrounding ranches. Local people crossed their community of wide-open spaces by horse, wagon, oxen-drawn cart, or by foot over roads winding through pasture lands.

Neighboring Pukalani developed as an agricultural and stock-raising area as well, expanding into pineapple upon the formation of the Pukalani Dairy and Pineapple Company in 1907. Just four years later, Haʻikū Fruit and Packing purchased the company's pineapple lands. The dairy and adjoining lands, on the other hand, sold to the Maui Agricultural Company for sugar cultivation. As a result, a sizeable plantation community developed at Keāhua, a few miles below Pukalani, complete with school, post office, and churches, all of which has now disappeared and been replaced with sugar cane.

Starting in 1915, Pukalani could boast a measure of glamor, as Maui polo enthusiasts transformed pasturage located between Pukalani and Haliʻimaile into a polo field, complete with stables and training facilities. Thereafter, crowds journeyed to Pukalani from throughout the island to delight in the excitement of top-notch polo.

In the 1920s and 1930s, residents in the Makawao/Pukalani vicinity patronized the Matsui Store, Komoda Store, Tam Chow Store, and T. Tanizaki Store, as well as the Makawao Theater, a meat market, slaughterhouse, two service stations, a harness shop and three blacksmiths. The Makawao Courthouse dispensed justice for a wide-ranging judicial district until it moved to Pāʻia in 1936, bequeathing its site to the new Makawao School. The population of this area in 1930 exceeded 1,200.

The community of Hāliʻimaile came into its own with the rise of the pineapple industry. In 1932, newly organized Maui Pineapple Company set up its headquarters there. As a typical self-contained plantation town, Hāliʻimaile provided its own store, theater, dispensary, recreational activities, and gymnasium.

Three Makawao churches have long served the community. Poʻokela Hawaiian Church pioneered in 1843. In 1917, well-known architect Charles W. Dickey designed a new Makawao Union Church, first established in 1870. Saint Joseph Church has served upcountry Catholics since 1911.

Pukalani, residential now and no longer rural, has grown by leaps and bounds in the past 25 years. Not far away by distance, Hāliʻimaile retains its plantation atmosphere and leisurely pace. Contemporary Makawao, on the other hand, suffers from popularity. Although congested, Makawao maintains its reputation as Maui's cowboy town, preserving its old-time flavor through the retention of its time-worn wooden buildings. Its spirit is most apparent when cowboys and cowgirls enliven the red, white and blue-draped town each July for the annual Makawao Rodeo and parade.

The Takeo Tanizaki family in front of the Tanizaki Store, 1929. This landmark store, which first opened its doors in 1927, has been rebuilt as the Pukalani Superette.

Makawao School, 1892. Principal Frederic Hardy and teachers Ellen Copp and B. Mundon stand behind their predominantly Hawaiian and Chinese students.

Makawao Union Church under construction, 1917.

Makawao town, 1979.

Makawao rodeo parade, late 1970s.

Hāliʻimaile plantation camp, 1930s. A Korean camp was located to the right.

The Crossroads USO during World War II. This building on Makawao Avenue has been reborn in various forms over the years - Tam Chow Store, Club Rodeo, and Casanova Italian Restaurant, just to name a few.

Hāliʻimaile Super Market, 1975. This center of activity in Hāliʻimaile has retaken its original name, Hāliʻimaile General Store.

Maui County Free Library bookmobile, 1930s. This travelling library served many small upcountry communities, including Kaupakulua and Keāhua.

HAʻIKŪ

Nature endowed the Hāmākua, or northern, coast of East Maui with features vital to Hawaiian prosperity and happiness. The area from Māliko to Nāʻiliʻilihāʻele Stream, just past Kailua, offered extensive coastal land ideal for growing wetland taro, as well as upper forest areas suitable for dryland taro cultivation. The climate also favored the growing of breadfruit, banana, arrowroot, yam, sugar cane, and ʻawa, a root used as a mild narcotic. Several small bays provided good fishing, and numerous gulches provided sloping land on which sweet potatoes thrived.

This abundant food supply supported a considerable Hawaiian population. And where Hawaiians dwelled, the missionaries were sure to follow. Haʻikū became the main outstation of the Wailuku missionary endeavor and the first site outside of Lahaina to have a church built of stone. Dedicated in 1840 and named Kalani Kahua, it preceded other nineteenth-century Protestant churches at Huelo and Paʻuwela, Catholic churches Saint Rita's in Haʻikū and Saint Ann's in Hāmākuapoko, and Buddhist missions at Hāmākuapoko and Paʻuwela.

Hawaiians of old knew sugar grew well in the Haʻikū area, a fact discovered by newcomers in the mid-1800s. The Haʻikū Sugar Company, organized by George Douglas in 1858, out-produced all others on Maui within four years of its founding. During that time, the company built its first mill across from its manager's home, a building which exists today at the Baldwin estate. Cane was ground there and shipped out of Māliko Bay for 23 years before the construction of a second and larger mill at Hāmākuapoko. The demise of the Hāmākuapoko mill coincided with Haʻikū Sugar Company's merger with Pāʻia Plantation. The resulting Maui Agricultural Company opened a new mill at Pāʻia in 1906, utilizing Hāmākuapoko's equipment. As an additional consequence of the merger, Haʻikū Sugar's ranching operation, called the Haʻikū Ranch, combined with Pāʻia Plantation's Grove Ranch under the latter name.

Although Haʻikū Sugar Company was the largest producer of sugar in the area, it was not the only one to capitalize on Haʻikū's favorable sugar growing climate. In the late 1870s, sugar also blossomed on the Lilikoʻi Plantation and the Huelo Plantation.

All eyes focused on Haʻikū in 1878, when sugar innovator Henry P. Baldwin forced his way through 17 miles of dense and rain-soaked Maui forest to finish the Hāmākua Ditch, Hawaiʻi's landmark irrigation project. In the same year, Haʻikū again made history when Charles H. Dickey stretched the first phone line in the islands between his Haʻikū home and his general store in Makawao.

Dickey, as well as the Baldwins, Beckwiths and other prominent haoles, or whites, sent their children to school at the Haʻikū Institute. For 20 years prior to the turn of the century, this small school educated a host of future leaders in Hawaiʻi.

The Huelo Plantation, by then called the Maui Sugar Company, went out of business in 1904, leaving the Maui Agricultural Company as the region's sole remaining sugar plantation and the area's biggest employer. A shortage of wheat flour during World War I prompted the company to plant corn extensively in Haʻikū. For a time its Haʻikū corn flour mill supplied the entire territory.

Although Maui Agricultural Company abandoned its Hāmākuapoko mill, Hāmākuapoko remained a thriving plantation community served by a theater, sports programs, a few small markets and a general store. Starting in 1913, Maui High School, the island's first co-educational secondary school, attracted students from central and East Maui.

Haʻikū and nearby communities also supported small stores supplying area residents who farmed, ranched, or maintained the Hāmākua Ditch. Four grammar schools served the district, teaching children at Haʻikū, Hāmākuapoko, Halehaku and Huelo.

In 1912, the territorial government and Henry P. Baldwin opened 2,000 acres of Kuiʻaha, Paʻuwela, and Kaupakulua for homesteading, but only to white Americans. Haoles from California, Honolulu and Maui claimed land, including a number of women. Some planted pineapple, while others experimented with diverse crops. Despite a promising beginning, dreams of creating an "American" settlement faded when discouraged homesteaders either leased their land to Japanese residents, or sold out. Within seven years, Japanese occupied almost all of the land intended for haoles.

The emerging pineapple industry influenced this transformation. Haʻikū Fruit and Packing Company solicited individuals to grow fruit for their cannery, an opportunity welcomed by Japanese seeking independence from plantation work. The Paʻuwela Pineapple Company followed the same practice, attracting additional contract growers. By 1930, pineapple planters and processors boosted the population of the region to almost 3,000.

Much has changed over the years. Hāmākuapoko's residents have dispersed. Small businesses exist where pineapple canneries once bustled. Residential development moves relentlessly forward. But not all is different. Fortunately, much of Haʻikū remains rural, supporting country pursuits - sugar, pineapple, farming and ranching.

Kuiʻaha railroad depot. Built in 1924, this depot served the pineapple cannery at Kuiʻaha.

Māliko Gulch, early 1900s.

125

Hāmākuapoko School, 1920s.

A picnic at Hāmākuapoko, 1890s. History does not reveal who these well-dressed revelers are, but possibly they are the supervisors of the Haʻiku Sugar Company Hāmākuapoko mill and plantation, with friends and family.

The village of Haʻiku, 1880s or 1890s.

WAILUKU

Wai, the Hawaiian word for water, figures prominently in Wailuku's history. Wailuku, along with Waikapū, Waiehu and Waiheʻe, composed an area called Nā Wai ʻEhā, or the four waters, whose streams and loʻi, or irrigated terraces, nourished the largest continuous region of wet taro cultivation in Hawaiʻi. This bounty sustained the second largest concentration of Hawaiians in precontact Maui.

The highest ranking aliʻi, or chiefs, derived power from these massive agricultural and human resources. Over the centuries, covetous rivals frequently transformed their desires for this wealth into battle plans. Around 1781, Hawaii island chief Kalaniʻōpuʻu made the last of repeated attempts to add Maui to his domain. He landed a large force at Māʻalaea, crossed Maui's isthmus and engaged Maui chief Kahekili's army at Wailuku. The Maui defenders routed Kalaniʻōpuʻu in a bloody two-day battle.

Less than ten years later, Kamehameha succeeded where Kalaniʻōpuʻu had failed, conquering Maui by defeating Kahekili in the battle of Kepaniwai in nearby ʻIao Valley. Kepaniwai, the water dam, refers to the damming of ʻIao Stream by the bodies of vanquished Maui warriors. In gratitude for his victory at ʻIao, Kamehameha is said to have offered a human sacrifice at Wailuku's Pihanakalani heaiu, or temple, one of many religious sites scattered throughout Nā Wai ʻEhā.

ʻIao Valley shelters one of the most revered sacred sites - the age-old cave known as Olopio, where only the highest rulers could be entombed. This royal ritual ceased with the internment of Maui chief Kekaulike, and knowledge of the cave's location has long been lost. Kekaulike's son, Kahekili, in deference to ʻIao's status, forbade commoners from travelling beyond the valley entrance. He himself maintained his court there, now the corner of Main and High Streets.

Some of the first foreigners to arrive in Wailuku established themselves in the sugar business in the 1820s, capitalizing on Wailuku's plentiful water. Others planted coffee at plantations in Wailuku and Waikapū. In the 1830s, missionaries brought not only education and religion to the community, but also initiated a cotton industry that was soon capable of creating hundreds of yards of cloth.

Not only businessmen tackled sugar-growing. In fact, missionaries planted cane in the heart of present-day Wailuku, and even King Kamehameha III raised sugar on the banks of ʻIao Stream. While many may have tried, in the long run only Wailuku Sugar Company succeeded. The company expanded into Waiheʻe and Waikapū in the 1880s, thus markedly influencing the physical and cultural development of the region. Their importation of plantation labor eventually altered the area's racial composition from mostly Hawaiian to predominantly Asian. This, in turn, caused a sizeable portion of Wailuku's plentiful taro patches to be transformed into rice paddies.

A century ago, dirt streets and wooden sidewalks laced Wailuku. Hawaiians on horseback filled corner lampposts with kerosene, their efforts negated when a strong Kona, or leeward, wind extinguished the lamps and plunged the streets into darkness. Hitching posts fronted every shop and residence, and barbers offered haircuts for a dime. Soda water purchased at the Maui Soda Works had to be imbibed without ice. And children and adults alike considered ice cream an exceptional treat, since it had to be ordered from Honolulu.

Although quiet by today's standards, turn-of-the-century Wailuku could rightfully claim to be prosperous and progressive. Business was looking up and population was on the rise. The founding of *The Maui News*, the island's only newspaper, made Wailuku all the more sophisticated. It was no surprise to the town's proud citizens when the territorial government selected Wailuku as the seat of the newly formed Maui County.

Worshippers with diverse beliefs and mother languages filled the pews of numerous churches. English-speaking haoles attended the Wailuku Union Church or the Church of the Good Shepherd and the Hawaiians, the Kaʻahumanu Church. The Japanese worshipped at the Hongwanji or Jodo missions, or the Japanese Christian Church, now called ʻIao Congregational Church. The Portuguese celebrated mass at Saint Anthony Church and the Chinese followed their religious beliefs at the Chinese Christian Church or one of two Chinese societies. Churchgoers from Waiheʻe and Waikapū attended services in their own communities.

As the business center of the island, Wailuku offered innumerable shops and a choice of hotels and banks. Several movie theaters satisfied the hunger of ardent movie fans, including the venerable ʻIao Theater, which opened in 1928. In 1948, 7,000 people made Wailuku their home.

Maui's pioneering social service agency, the Alexander House Settlement, provided kindergartens, English classes for immigrants, programs in health and nutrition, and many other forms of assistance. The settlement, also the center of Wailuku social life, sponsored concerts, dances, and socials, in addition to providing a gymnasium, swimming pool and organized athletic leagues. An early settlement reading room evolved into the Maui County Library. The Alexander House Settlement bettered the lives of thousands of Wailuku and other Maui residents from 1901 until its demise in the late 1940s.

Several structures with significant architectural value grace the streets of Wailuku. H. L. Kerr designed the Wailuku Courthouse, Wailuku's oldest government build-

ing, which opened in 1907. Hawaiʻi's premier architect, Charles W. Dickey, built the Wailuku Elementary School in 1904, the Wailuku Library in 1929, and, in the 1930s, the Territorial Office Building and the Wailuku Sugar Company Manager's home. William d'Esmond, another noted architect, designed the Saint Anthony School and the County Office Building in the early 1920s, as well as numerous residences. The former Territorial Office Building, located between Kaʻahumanu Church and the Wailuku Library, has housed many

State agencies over time, while the former County Office Building has evolved from Police Department headquarters to a County annex.

The Wailuku area's fascinating history can be discovered, or rediscovered, by a stroll through its streets and hidden lanes, or by hiking into its celebrated valleys. As in ancient times, Wailuku retains much of its status as a population and government center and upholds its reputation as a combat site. The only difference is that, today, legal battles in Wailuku's courthouse replace the bloodshed of old.

ʻIao Valley, circa 1910.

Market Street during World War II.

Wailuku, with Saint Anthony High School and Church in foreground, Wailuku Sugar mill in background, 1940s.

Market Street, 1890s.

Taxi service business card, 1940s.

Main Street, 1930s.

Enos store, early 1900s.

Wailuku in 1898.

ʻĪao Theater, 1930s. This theater was one of many that entertained Wailuku residents.

Waikapū, 1890s.

Fish market, 1910.

131

KAHULUI

Twenty-six pili grass houses sheltered the entire population of Kahului in 1837. These Hawaiians living close to the ocean relied upon fishing the coastal waters for much of their food.

For many years, Kahului's most important resource was its nearby fishponds. About 250 years ago, a Hawaiian ali'i named Kapi'ioho'okalani began construction of two ponds separated by a stone wall. These twin ponds named Kanahā and Mau'oni supplied mullet during the season when fishing the sea was forbidden. Up to the early 1900s, mullet still flourished there, and people swam in its continually refreshed spring waters. Over the years, materials dredged from Kahului Harbor filled in large sections of what was by then simply called Kanahā Pond, and eventually its outlet to the sea was blocked.

Modern Kahului began to develop in the 1860s in response to the needs of the emerging sugar industry in neighboring Wailuku. A warehouse, stores, wheelwright and blacksmith shops centered around the harbor. Before the century ended, Kahului sported a new customhouse, a saloon, Chinese restaurants, a railroad and a small population of residents. A visitor in 1898 was not impressed, "the first glance of Kahului is by no means inspiring." Inspiring or not, Kahului provided appropriate support for its prime industry - shipping.

Kahului's residents lost both their lives and homes during a bubonic plague outbreak in 1900. In an effort to contain the epidemic, officials burned down the Chinatown area, displacing Chinese, Japanese and Hawaiian residents. As an added measure, authorities encircled the entire town with corrugated iron rat-proof fences, successfully ending the plague menace.

Kahului thrived in the twentieth century as Maui's primary harbor and as a commercial center. Residents found employment with the Kahului Railroad, or as dock workers, clerks, cannery workers, or in nearby cane fields. Numerous and varied businesses lined the streets, many of them Japanese. The largest stores catering to the Japanese trade were the Japanese Mercantile Company, Maui Shokai and M. Kobayashi, K. Ikeda and J. Onishi stores. Hawaiian Commercial & Sugar Company operated two large stores in town, a retail operation called Kahului Store, located on Pu'unēnē Avenue, and the other a wholesale operation named Pu'unēnē Store, which supplied the network of plantation camp stores.

Both commercial establishments and homes filled the area along the ocean where hotels are now located, as well as across the street from the current Kahului Shopping Center to the Maui Mall, and down Pu'unēnē Avenue to the former Maui County Fairgrounds. Distinctively named plantation camps, such as Raw Fish Camp, Filipino Camp and Store Camp spread across the patchwork town. Intermittent stands of kiawe, or mesquite, added to the landscape mix.

Although a commercial center, the pace of life at Kahului was still slow in the 1930s. Everyone walked everywhere, whether it be to the horseraces at the fairgrounds, the ocean to fish, the Kahului Theater, or bon dances. Kahului's earliest churches, the Kahului Union Church, Christ the King and the Kahului Hongwanji Mission reflected the community's racial blend.

After World War II, when the Kahului Development Company announced its intention to build houses for sale to HC&S employees, long-time camp occupants responded eagerly. Before, few workers could aspire to home ownership. Now, for an average cost of $7,250, they could fulfill their dreams. Accurately reflecting this widespread enthusiasm, the developers called the new town Dream City. A lucky family moved in to the first house in 1950. Within a year, the "modern" Kahului Shopping Center opened its doors to business. The founding of Dream City led to the decline and closing of plantation camps and stores, and to the rise of Kahului as a major population area with up-to-date shopping facilities.

To travel back in time, one only has to pause a moment, look up at the coconut palms on Kahului's main thoroughfare, and know that these same trees lined Kahului Railroad tracks and shaded a port town much different from today.

Construction of Pier One, then called the Maui Wharf, 1923.

Kahului waterfront, 1870s to 1880s.

Corner of Puʻunēnē and Main Street, Kahului, 1940. Charles W. Dickey designed the Baldwin Bank on right in 1931. Note Masonic Temple in background.

Main Street, Kahului, around 1910, with Masonic Temple on right.

Puʻunēnē Avenue store flooded by 1946 tidal wave.

M. Kobayashi Cash Store, Puʻunēnē Avenue, 1920s, one of five large stores catering to the Japanese trade.

Kahului Railroad wharf, 1923.

HĀNA

Hāna rightfully claims a place of highest honor in Hawaiian legend and history. For centuries, chiefs of both Maui and the nearby island of Hawai'i fought bitterly to possess Hāna, its natural abundance and beauty making it a desirable sanctuary in peace as well as war.

Warring rulers particularly valued Hāna's volcanic point, called Ka'uiki, since it provided a formidable fortress for defense against rivals. Ka'uiki is also esteemed as the home of the demigod Māui, for which the island was named, and as the birthplace of the revered queen, Ka'ahumanu.

Hawaiians densely settled in the Hāna and neighboring Ko'olau districts, making them two of the five most populous areas on the island. The Hāna area primarily supported itself through dryland taro cultivation complemented by fishing. It also earned a reputation for the quality of the narcotic root called 'awa that grew there. In contrast, the many Hawaiian villages along the Ko'olau, or northeastern, coast grew wetland taro irrigated by streams that flowed from rain-drenched mountains through lush valleys. The frequent rains favoring Ko'olau distinguished the coastal region as the wettest in all Hawai'i.

In ancient times, Wailua Nui, a populous and productive village along the Ko'olau coast, contrasted sharply with the barren lava-covered Ke'anae peninsula. In response,

Ke'anae's ruler implemented an ambitious and self-serving plan. He forced his subjects to carry heavily laden baskets packed with soil from the mountains to create lowland taro patches, an immense chore taking years to complete. This Herculean effort expanded agriculture which supported an increased population, and thereby bolstered the shrewd chief's political power.

When missionaries Daniel Conde and Mark Ives arrived in 1837, they estimated that 3,000 Hawaiians lived in Hāna. The area remained overwhelmingly Hawaiian, even after Westerners introduced sugar cultivation in 1851. Although this first attempt at establishing a sugar industry failed when the mill burned down, a Dane named August Unna revived the idea in 1862 and founded the Hāna Plantation. By the 1870s, Hāna village sported a courthouse, a school and two stores.

The Hāna district, however, was destined to change. The shortage of Hawaiian labor at Hāna Plantation (renamed the Ka'elekū Sugar Company by the new owner M. S. Grinbaum in 1905), as well as additional plantations subsequently established at Hāmoa, Nāhiku and Kīpahulu, required the recruitment of various ethnic groups. Newcomers also joined the Hawaiian populace in ranching and later in pineapple work. Each small community in the Hāna district sustained at least one small general store, a schoolhouse and Protestant and Catholic churches.

Mass production of the automobile on the mainland opened the door for a rubber industry in distant Nāhiku. The Nāhiku Rubber Company planted rubber trees in 1905, soon followed by the Ko'olau Rubber Company and the Hawaiian American Rubber Company. Although these enterprises optimistically planted thousands of acres, a decline in the price of rubber doomed the infant industry by 1915. The East Maui rubber industry came to life briefly only once again due to World War II shortages.

The recruitment of plantation labor remained a persistent problem in such a remote area, prompting an unusual approach during World War I. Government authorities in Honolulu paroled several Germans classified as alien enemies, sent them to an internment camp at Kīpahulu Plantation, and required them to wield a hoe.

The year 1926 marked a turning point for the Hāna district. Completion of the Belt Road, now named Hāna Highway, made it possible to travel by automobile from central Maui all the way to Kīpahulu, eliminating reliance on the weekly steamer for contact with the world. The forging of this unpaved road through precipitous cliffs and jungle gulches had been a monumental task and clearly deserved a Hāna-style dedication - a lū'au lasting for two days.

By 1930, more than 4,000 people made the region their home. Many Hawaiians preserved the ways of old Hawai'i through traditional agriculture and fishing. The majority of the population, however, lived in Hāna because of work available at Kaʻeleku Sugar Company.

In the late 1930s, callers to the community lodged either at the Hāna Hotel or the Omsted Court. Visitors and local folk alike ate at the Hāna or T. Nakahashi restaurants. The plantation-owned Hāna Store housed the self-contained community's other necessities - a post office, bank, lumber yard, ice plant and gas station. Shoppers could also patronize the local Hasegawa or C. Ah Lung stores, or take advantage of round-trip bus service via the eight-passenger vehicles of the Hāna Bus Line, which shuttled people twice-weekly between the Hāna Barber Shop and Ah Fook's in Kahului.

The complexion of the community changed in 1944, when San Francisco capitalist Paul Fagan purchased Kaʻeleku, closed down sugar operations, and converted most of the land to ranch use. The closure of the plantation forced many workers to depart for opportunities elsewhere.

Fagan realized his dream of building a modern resort hotel three years later when he opened what is now known as the Hotel Hāna-Maui on the same plot of land used by Hāna's first missionaries. Some of the hotel's first and most memorable guests, the Fagan-owned San Francisco Seals baseball team, arrived amidst fanfare. As Pacific Coast League champs, the Seals charged Hāna with big-time thrills during a too-brief, three-week training stint.

Maui's tidal wave of 1946 hit hardest on the Hāna coast. The unexpected tsunami destroyed Hāmoa, left Keʻanae with only its church, and killed 13 people. But Hāna's spirit was not long diminished. Even through population decline, a see-saw economy, and natural disasters, Hāna has survived. Most importantly, Hāna has retained its native traditions and its Hawaiian heart.

Hanā Bay, circa 1900.

Kaupō Saloon, around 1890s.

Hāna, 1883.

Ditch trail to Hāna, around 1915. It was not until 1926, when the Belt Road was completed, that automobiles could travel from central Maui all the way to Hāna.

Hasegawa Store, on left, 1940s.

HALEAKALĀ

Hawaiians knew that Pele the volcano goddess could unleash her fiery fury from Haleakalā at any time. Despite this threat, ancient sojourners sought prized resources available at the mountain's summit, travelling to Maui's highest point to hunt birds, to conduct religious ceremonies and to gather dense rock for adzes. According to tradition, Hawaiians often ventured to isolated and distant areas to inter their dead, making the crater a desirable burial site, even for those as far away as the island of Hawai'i.

Hawaiians also used Haleakalā as a shortcut. In order to more easily traverse East Maui from north to south, Hawaiians created a thoroughfare through the summit and out Kaupō Gap by laying out a road paved with smooth rocks. It is believed, however, that robbers sometimes made this trade route perilous.

A party of three missionaries provided the first written account of an ascent to the mountain top in 1828, followed 13 years later by a report submitted by Charles Wilkes of the United States Exploring Expedition who reconnoitered the area. Nineteenth-century visitors, intrigued by early accounts, travelled many extraordinarily rough miles to reach their destination. Once there, caves offered the only overnight shelter, as the first primitive rest house wasn't built until 1894. Travellers, though exhausted by their strenuous effort to get to the top, were well rewarded, finding Haleakalā's crater, as one admirer described it, "awe-inspiring in its sublimity."

Thoughtlessly harming the landscape they came to admire, souvenir collectors commonly picked leaves of the unusual 'āhinahina, or silversword, to decorate a hat, or plucked whole plants for sport. One enterprising Mauian even advertised specimens for sale nationally through *Popular Science Monthly*. Free-roaming wild goats and bullocks, abetted by domestic cattle pastured in the crater by Haleakalā Ranch, wreaked further havoc. Despite the depletion of the sensitive plants, Maui citizens gathered several gunnysacks' worth of 'āhinahina's silky silver leaves in 1911 and subsequent years to decorate floats representing Maui in Honolulu Floral Parades.

No one was more enthusiastic about Haleakalā's beauty than Olinda resident Worth Aiken. For the first 30 years of the century, Aiken operated a Haleakalā horse transportation and guide business based at his home, Idlewilde. Only two to three tourists at most, however, attempted the rugged trip up the mountain each month in 1914, a fact distressing to Maui promoters.

As a consequence, Aiken and other civic-minded citizens lobbied successfully for Haleakalā to unite with the volcano region of the island of Hawai'i in the formation of Hawai'i National Park. Earning national park status in 1921 helped to bring Haleakalā to the public's attention, but accessibility was still a problem. The age of the automobile had arrived, yet experiencing the pleasures at Haleakalā's peak still required horses. Fortunately, federal funding made the dream of an auto road possible.

The day in 1935 that Haleakalā Highway opened was momentous! The Territorial Legislature adjourned so the politicians could attend the dedication, businesses closed, NBC broadcast the ceremony nationwide, and an astounding 1,600 people christened the winding automobile road in relative comfort. In the second year of the highway's existence, ten times that number drove to the top of the mountain.

In the 1930s, just as today, stalwart sightseers enjoyed descending into the crater. Hikers or horse riders could cover much of the moonlike expanse in a day trip, or stay overnight either in tents or in three Civilian Conservation Corps-built cabins. Guides made the trip even more interesting and comfortable. Legendary guide Frank Freitas spent 50 years showing off Haleakalā's special features to curious visitors, including royalty and movie stars.

During World War II, thousands of isle-based servicemen made the trek, although access to the summit was limited to daylight hours. They were not the only military personnel to experience the mountain, as the United States Army maintained a camp high on its slopes. After the war, the Haleakalā Mountain Lodge remodeled the abandoned Army buildings in order to provide rest, food and tour accommodations for park visitors.

In 1961, Haleakalā became an independent national park. Since that time, the park has acquired additional land, improved its trails and, through conservation efforts, replenished the threatened 'āhinahina and the nēnē, or Hawaiian goose. And of utmost importance, the volcano, which has been dormant since 1790, has kept on sleeping.

Hardy adventurers seeking shelter in cave, 1890s.

Wedding party in Haleakalā crater adorned with silverswords, around 1890s.

On right, Lawrence "Chu" Baldwin and friend, around 1925, enjoying Hawaiian snow.

An early rest house provided for visitors to Haleakalā, early 1920s.

KĪHEI AND MĀKENA

Like the pristine ocean that defines the area, Maui's southern coastline community from Māʻalaea through Kīhei to Mākena has experienced a marked ebb and flow over time. For hundreds of years, Hawaiians lived comfortably in scattered villages, fishing the sea, maintaining fishponds, and trading with upland areas for agricultural products. The outside world intruded into this Polynesian setting when the French explorer La Perouse arrived at Keoneʻōʻio for a fleeting visit in 1786, making his mark on history as the first non-Hawaiian on Maui's shores.

Forty years later, Protestant missionaries set up shop on the coast with clear intent - to alter Hawaiian traditional life through Christian religion. And they succeeded. Keawalaʻi Church at Mākena was founded in 1832, followed by churches at Kanaio, Keawakapu, and Kalepolepo.

Foreign seamen and traders who pursued fortune, rather than God's favor, were no less influential than the missionaries. Among these entrepreneurs was craftsman and businessman John Halstead, who settled in the village of Kalepolepo in 1849, drawn there by the money to be made in buying and selling Kula produce. Halstead's store occupied the first floor of his three-story residence, a landmark building known as the Koa House. This singular structure attracted notice for nearly a hundred years because

much of its exterior wood, as well as its furniture and shelving, was constructed of richly colored and textured koa wood.

The company Halstead kept provides proof of his stature during this boom period of Maui history. No less than four Hawaiian monarchs visited him over time at the Koa House. Halstead's prosperity, however, was dependent on whaling and the California potato trade and, when they came to an end, so did the Koa House and Kalepolepo village.

Events on the mainland United States again influenced South Maui when the supply of cotton to the northern states halted during the Civil War. In response, entrepreneurs planted cotton extensively throughout the Mākena area, ginned the resulting crops, and sent them off to the textile mills of New England. Although exports ceased after the war, the idea of a cotton industry did not die. Sixty years later, Heiyamon Suda revived the industry at his Kīhei Cotton Factory.

Before the introduction of the kiawe, or mesquite tree, Maui's southern coastal vista was more open and, of course, less detrimental to barefoot beachgoers. Bathers enjoyed various swimming spots, the same beaches formalized as parks today. The military used these beaches for military exercises during World War II, some of which still retain concrete pillboxes as relics of that era.

Mākena, a bustling port in the nineteenth century, ranked second

only to Lahaina in economic importance on Maui. Inter-island steamers packed their holds with cargoes of pineapples, eggs, poultry and vegetables, in addition to barrels of sugar and live cattle from ʻUlupalakua. Up until 1912, each and every steamer en route from Honolulu to Hilo called at Mākena. Thereafter, Mākena landing handled shipments for ʻUlupalakua Ranch only.

At the turn of the century, South Maui welcomed the fledgling Kīhei Plantation, complete with a store, hospital, and residential camps for its workers. The operation did not prosper, however, and financial failure forced the company to sell out to Hawaiian Commercial & Sugar Company in 1908.

Paralleling its neighbors, the Māʻalaea area has been in and out of the limelight. Although not as important a port as Mākena, Māʻalaea landing served as an active shipping point until 1906. And, despite its reputation for strong winds, the territorial government chose Māʻalaea as the site for Maui's first official airport, opened in 1930. Eight years later, the airport closed, because newer and larger planes required more distance from the West Maui mountains for safe takeoffs.

During the first decades of the twentieth century, there was little to attract people to South Maui, other than the commercial harvest of kiawe and good fishing, and by 1930, only 350 people made Kīhei their home. The government offered 11 beach lots for sale in 1932 with

141

the hope of spurring development of a desirable residential district, but few paid notice, and only six sold. By 1950, farm land could be purchased for $225 an acre and residential lots sold for a mere five to ten cents a square foot to the occasional person desiring dry, dusty Kīhei property. The sparse population patronized a meager number of local businesses such as the M. Tomokiyo Store and Roadside Inn, the Kīhei Store, and Bill Azeka's grocery store, begun in 1950.

Since the 1950s, the Kīhei area has undergone tremendous growth, with an explosion of condominiums, luxury hotels, shopping centers, restaurants, homes and highways. Once again, Maui's southern coast has seen its fortunes rise, this time perhaps for good.

Kīhei Wharf and lighthouse, 1913, the year the wharf was constructed.

Birds-eye view of Kīhei, with Kama'ole Beach in foreground, 1940s.

Driving cattle to long boat for further transport on steamer to Honolulu, Mākena, early 1920s.

Cowboys moving cattle into surf at Mākena, 1940. This old style of transporting cattle was revived, due to a surplus of stock for a brief time in 1940.

Kihei Plantation Co., Ltd.

Kihei Plantation's efforts at sugar-growing ended in 1908, when it was sold to Hawaiian Commercial & Sugar Company.

Koa House, Kalepolepo, 1920s. Halstead descendent Charlotte Halstead, at far left, lived in the house until her death in 1937. This Kihei landmark, constructed primarily of koa, was destroyed in 1946.

KAHAKULOA

The sparsely settled and secluded valley of Kahakuloa was not always so tranquil. In fact, by ancient Hawaiian standards, the area was jampacked. Kahakuloa owes its status as one of the five most populous sites in precontact Maui to 'Eke crater in the West Maui mountains. 'Eke, which occasionally outranks Wai'ale'ale on Kaua'i as the most rain-drenched site in Hawai'i, pours much of its abundance down Kahakuloa Stream. Its vigorous waters allowed Hawaiians to intensively cultivate taro, arrowroot, sweet potatoes, wauke, or mulberry, and olonā, a plant used for fiber, far back into the valley.

Although not at its peak when Protestant and Catholic missionaries arrived in the 1830s and 1840s, Kahakuloa still supported a substantial Hawaiian community. Like other communities on Maui, Kahakuloa tragically declined in population throughout the 1800s because of disease and outmigration, but, unlike others, its populace was not replaced through significant immigration of foreigners.

In horse-and-buggy days, Kahakuloa's beauty attracted many Mauians for lū'aus and other social gatherings. Ironically, Kahakuloa's popularity as a gathering place declined when the automobile came into use. The unpaved road that linked the community to the outside world proved too perilous for cars and drivers to negotiate.

In the early 1930s, a novel method was used by parties of tourists who wanted to circle the island despite this near-impassable road. A group of tourists would divide into two, with one-half taking the trip by automobile to Honokōhau. They then would wait until their counterparts reached the end of the paved road on the Wailuku side and crossed the remaining difficult section on horseback. At the meeting place, the riders exchanged horses for the waiting cars, both parties proceeding the rest of the way around the island.

Ranching and small farms provided livelihoods for many in the district during the early part of the twentieth century. In 1922, the Pa'uwela Pineapple Company began to transform sections of the Kahakuloa area into pineapple fields with its initial purchase of Marshall Ranch. Libby, McNeill & Libby took over Pa'uwela and its Kahakuloa holdings in 1926. Independent Japanese planters, in order to transport their fruit more efficiently, constructed an automobile road from their fields through the village and up to the main coastal road in 1930. That same year, 274 people inhabited the Kahakuloa area. Several homesteaders, mostly Portuguese, joined the community when they acquired land in the vicinity in the early 1940s.

By 1945, 20 or so Hawaiian families lived in Kahakuloa village, sustaining themselves with home-grown produce, rice, and fish from the sea. Mango, breadfruit, banana, mountain apple, and java plum trees provided their abundance, along with family taro patches. Simple dwellings nestled among luxuriant vegetation created an idyllic landscape.

Throughout the 1930s and 1940s, Kahakuloa School's one teacher also acted as the principal, secretary and custodian to a class of 20 or so students in grades one to eight. During this period a small grass shack located on the school grounds stood as a symbol of Kahakuloa's ancient Hawaiian roots.

Time has changed Kahakuloa. Many residents commute to jobs outside the valley and Kahakuloa School is closed. The Kahakuloa Protestant and Saint Francis Xavier churches welcome worshippers only once a month. Kahakuloa remains, however, one of the very few Hawaiian communities in the State and undoubtedly one of its most picturesque.

Kahakuloa School, 1927.

WORLD WAR II - MILITARY DELUGE

World War II not only knocked on Maui's door, it lingered on the lānai. Men in uniform outnumbered local residents four to one during the war years, as 200,000 soldiers, sailors, marines and seabees flooded the community for training, as well as rest between missions. Some units stayed only a short time, some longer, but each impacted the rural, plantation-oriented community.

The military invaded Maui in 1940, when the United States Navy began construction of a naval air station at the site of the newly built community airport at Pu'unēnē in order to provide a base for the first military unit to be stationed on Maui, Utility Squadron Three. At the time of the 1941 attack on Pearl Harbor, 150 Navy men and 7 officers, plus a few Army personnel, called Pu'unēnē Naval Air Station home.

The advent of war spurred the rapid expansion of the naval air station as a site for the training and staging of aircraft carrier air groups. In 1945, 206 officers and 2,465 enlisted men and women were assigned to the station, plus 700 additional men in transient squadrons, and 271 aircraft.

Despite its expansion, the naval station at Pu'unēnē proved inadequate to meet the urgent need for training of large numbers of pilots and crews required for the Pacific Theater. In response, by early 1943

the Navy had transformed yet more cane fields into the Kahului Naval Air Station to provide a training site for two to three more air groups.

Aviators sped through concentrated training, including daily patrols, predawn launches, torpedo, rocket and bombing attacks, gunnery firings, carrier landing practices, intercepts, radar and oxygen hops, radar approaches, mine laying flights, camera and mapping flights, and survival lectures. Mauians lived with the din of airplane engines around the clock.

This intense instruction prepared the navy men for high-risk assignments in the Pacific. After experiencing the tension of combat, the aviators would once again return to Maui, with elation in their heart and celebration on their mind. One squadron returned from action in the Solomon Islands to see the rooftops around Pu'unēnē carrying messages of welcome spelled out in flowers. The most famous of the United States Navy air groups used Maui as a staging area and, therefore, the island became well known in naval aviation circles.

The Navy's presence was not limited to Pu'unēnē and Kahului. A Demolition Training Station at Kīhei developed underwater demolition teams and furthered knowledge of anti-mine cables used on warships. And the Navy and Marines could not have functioned without the aid of four Navy Seabee battalions stationed wherever their construction skills were needed.

Also contributing to the military

effort, a Coast Guard contingent of 500 hundred officers and men kept watch over the port of Kahului. Established on Maui in 1943, the Coast Guard patrolled piers, regulated fishing, protected sugar shipments and, in co-operation with the Army and Marines, guarded the docks and ships when valuable war cargoes were unloaded.

Then, the Marines landed. Camp Maui, a huge base camp in the Kokomo area of upcountry Maui, was erected in 1944 as a refuge for almost 20,000 men of the Fourth Marine Division between battles in the Pacific. The Marines revered Camp Maui as a site for rest and recreation, even though many activities, including nightly open-air movies, were often experienced in the rain and mud.

Maui's varied terrain from mountain to sea provided excellent training grounds for these fighting men heading for the South Pacific. Marines trained all over the island, hiking through Haleakalā crater and rehearsing amphibious maneuvers on Maui's southern beaches from Mā'alaea Bay to Mākena. Workers on Maui's plantations prepared the Marines for the rigors of fighting in the sugar fields of Saipan and Tinian by teaching them how to maneuver through the dense cane and how to fight cane fires.

The Marines won their way into the hearts of the people and became known as "Maui's Own." The sentiment was mutual. When the men of the Fourth Division emerged triumphant at Iwo Jima, they named the first street built there "Maui Boulevard." And, when they returned to Maui after the costly battle, the Maui community turned out en masse at Kahului Harbor to welcome their warriors home. The local community showed their aloha for the last time by providing a heroes' send-off when the Fourth Marine Division departed in late 1945.

The presence of the United States Army added to the mix of military. When the war began, Maui's army contingent consisted of a battalion of local troops of the 299th Infantry of the Hawai'i National Guard. That was soon to change. Early 1942 brought the arrival of the 27th Division, followed by units of the 40th Division and the units of the 33rd Division, all of which saw action in the South Pacific. The last to arrive was the 98th Mohawk Division. Army units occupied camps at locations throughout Maui, including Kula, Paukūkalo, and the Maui County Fairgrounds. They operated two hospitals, one newly constructed in Waikapū and one based in the former Makawao School. The Army, along with the Navy and the Marines, also utilized Maui's nearly 50 military training sites.

Military life on Maui was not all work. USOs beckoned servicemen at Makawao, Pā'ia, Ha'ikū, Kahului, Wailuku, and Camp Maui. A parade of local hula dancers, singers and dance bands, as well as big Hollywood names, including Bob Hope, entertained the troops. Sports leagues offered diversion, high-lighted by occasional visits by major league baseball players who challenged Maui's best.

Local residents generously welcomed military men into their homes between missions. Particularly noted for her hospitality during these years, Alexa von Tempsky Zabriskie entertained more than 20,000 officers and men at her ranch Erehwon, on the slopes of Haleakalā. Maui families were the last civilians many of these men saw before meeting their deaths in the Pacific.

The fateful four years of World War II left a legacy for modern-day Maui. Tangible evidence of the Pu'unēnē Naval Air Station remains in view between Kīhei and Pu'unēnē, and concrete pillboxes, bunkers, and bomb casings spot the contemporary landscape from Kula to Mākena. Although the Kahului Naval Air Station is gone, its location is still commonly called Naska, the military contraction for Naval Air Station - KAhului. Former members of the Fourth Marine Division keep Camp Maui's memory alive through a park at its former site. And the least tangible remnants of the pervasive military presence, but the most important, are the friendships established between local people and military men that are maintained to this day.

1942 cartoon appearing in **The Maui News** *depicting life on Market Street, Wailuku.*

147

The Fourth Marine Division at Kokomo. The knoll at the right is still called Giggle Hill, as its peak was the site of off-duty activities of marines and local girls.

Airplanes at the Naval Air Station, Kahului, 1943-1946.

Maui residents viewing United States Navy maneuvers through barbed wire strung on South Maui beach. Because of military censorship, photos such as this one are seldom seen.

WORLD WAR II - LIFE AT HOME

"Sub Shells Kahului!" screamed the *Maui News* headline. Luckily, the Japanese submarine that sneaked within range of Kahului on December 15, 1941, had bad aim. Two shells landed in the harbor, and three grazed the Maui Pineapple Company cannery. Once again on December 31, a Japanese submarine wasted its ammunition, first undershooting into the harbor and then overshooting the town in the direction of Puʻunēnē. The death toll from both these attacks amounted to only one - a chicken, and property damage to the cannery proved minor. Peace of mind took a harder hit.

More evidence of Japanese aggression surfaced on December 21, when 30 survivors of a submarine attack on the Matson freighter *Lahaina* came to shore at Spreckelsville after traveling 800 miles in a harrowing 11-day journey that cost the lives of four crewmen. Maui again directly confronted war in early 1942, when a Japanese torpedo sank the Army transport *Royal T. Frank* within sight of land between Maui and Hawaiʻi, killing 24 men. A local boat rescued the survivors and delivered them to Hāna.

These experiences so close to home made the local community more determined than ever to contribute to the war effort. The Territory of Hawaiʻi boasted the best war bond record in the nation, and Maui proudly contributed to that honor, often doubling its quota. Everyone, young and old, worked long hours to fill the desperate need for civilian labor. High school students attended classes only four days a week, freeing them for a day of labor in the sugar or pineapple fields, or wherever they were needed.

The Maui Planters Association explained their contributions with the statement, "Uncle Sam's fighting men and the Sugar Industry are Comrades against the Axis!", reminding all that sugar converted to industrial alcohol became explosives, and that sugar gave soldiers essential energy for the challenges of the battle front.

Other local patriots formed the Maui Volunteers to guard vital installations, to keep peace in plantation camps, and to prepare for possible attack. Army-trained and uniformed in khaki, the men practiced and patrolled after long hours in plantation jobs. Also concerned with the island's defense, cowboys guarded the vast Maui ranch lands on horseback as members of the Maui Mounted Patrol.

The threat of invasion motivated the territorial governor to place Hawaiʻi under martial law two days after the declaration of war, resulting in the establishment of a Maui Military District headquartered in Wailuku School. The Army replaced civilian authority in almost everything, including curfews, driving, consumer prices, and the local news media. A military court presided over offenses ranging from traffic violations to serious crime. Army judges ruled expeditiously, but sometimes harshly.

Citizens of Maui could not forget the war for long, for they were bombarded by reminders. Military men on leave crowded the streets of every town. Shoeshine boys, restaurants, photo studios and lei sellers mushroomed in Wailuku and other areas to cater to the military trade. And defense measures radically altered the island's appearance - camouflage paint coated buildings, including Baldwin High School and Kaʻahumanu Church, barbed wire lined beaches, and blackout paint shrouded windows.

To meet the demands of war, each and every person's help was critical, including the one-third of Maui's population that was of Japanese ancestry. The large number of Japanese residents made mass internment such as had occurred on the mainland impractical. Unfortunately, however, not all island Japanese escaped this fate. Authorities arrested Japanese language teachers, priests and others with close ties to their homeland, held them in the Wailuku Jail or a site in Haʻikū, and ultimately sent them for internment on Oʻahu or the mainland.

Although most Japanese were not interned, they bore the burden of unfounded suspicion, primarily from the mainland United States. Hollywood fanned the flames of anti-Japanese emotion when the 1942 film *Air Force* depicted local Japanese residents machine-gunning an American bomber from the hills above the Maui airport at the same time the forces of Hirohito were assaulting Pearl Harbor.

Countering the distrust of their country's leaders, the Japanese American community contributed unfailingly to every aspect of the war effort. They formed a patriotic organization called the Maui Emergency Service Committee, which conducted blood drives, promoted a "Speak American" campaign, and sponsored a Kiawe Corps to clear the thorn-plagued and stubborn kiawe thickets from Maui's southern beaches. This arduous task supplied wood to the military and cleared land for military purposes. The Emergency Service Committee also organized a military recruitment drive, which proved unnecessary, as young Japanese men flooded the enlistment office as soon as they were eligible.

Mauians of all races and backgrounds pulled together to back the war effort and to show their patriotism. And, when the war ended, one and all shared an identical feeling of jubilation and relief.

Maui girl in gas mask, prepared for invasion of island. Even babies were issued gas masks, called bunny masks.

Maui News headline in 1941, reporting an attack by a Japanese submarine on December 15.

Lahaina storefront showing photos of Maui servicemen, as encouragement to buying war bonds.

Napoleon Agasid, manager of the Maui branch of the Filipino Federation of America, and co-worker, 1940s, promoting the sale of war bonds.

WORLD WAR II - SACRIFICE IN SERVICE

Mauians' eagerness to serve their country surpassed the military's capacity to enlist them. Men of Portuguese, Hawaiian, Puerto Rican, Filipino, Chinese, Caucasian, and Korean ancestry responded readily at the call to arms after Pearl Harbor and, once enlisted, amassed a memorable record in every branch of the military. Maui's women also served honorably in the Women's Army Corps. But the equally patriotic Japanese had to wait.

After the declaration of war with Japan, the United States government barred Japanese American men from enlisting. At the same time, the military struggled with a dilemma. What were they going to do with Japanese soldiers already serving successfully? The Army's solution was to test these soldiers' commitment by gathering them into an all-Japanese 100th Infantry Battalion, and sending them into heavy combat in Europe.

Due to this unit's remarkable combat record and the unswerving allegiance of the Japanese civilian community, the call finally went out for Japanese American enlistment in the United States Army in 1943. Because so many earnest young men flocked to Maui's recruitment office, the Army raised its quota. Those selected from throughout the islands formed the 442nd Regimental Combat Team. Innumerable acts of bravery on the battlefields of France and Italy earned this gallant group of Americans the distinction of being one of the Army's most decorated units.

In a letter home, Private First Class Tamotsu Hanida spoke for his fellow Japanese soldiers when he promised, "While I am standing up I am going to do my utmost best to push the enemies back and help win this war...the boys from Hawaii are not going to fail you people back home." Within weeks, the 24-year-old Kula resident lay dead on an Italian battlefield. At a posthumous ceremony honoring his son, Shohei Hanida expressed his one wish, "that he could have lived a little longer so he could have fought for his country that much longer."

Men of every race put their lives on the line for their country. Representing countless island heroes, Lieutenant Wilbert Yee spent two years in a German prisoner of war camp, and Staff Sergeant John Gomes Jr. flew on numerous combat missions over Europe as a bombardier. Sergeant Valentine Kekipi earned Maui's first Silver Star for heroic conduct in New Guinea, and Major Gordon Walker received a Navy Cross for courage in the Pacific. Few Maui's soldiers served honorably in as many diversified Pacific campaigns as Sergeant Theodoro Nitura.

Scores of others risked their lives, but lost. One hundred and twenty-four Maui men met death in Europe and in the Pacific in defense of their country, their race, and their island.

Henry "Buddy" Bissen of Wailuku, Ernest Damkroger of Wailuku and George Wong of Pā'ia, three of 124 Maui men who gave their lives for their country.

Military recruiting advertisement appearing in The Maui News, *1943.*

Jiro Suzawa of Lahaina at sendoff to military service, 1943. Suzawa was a member of the highly decorated 442nd Regimental Combat Team, one of many who made the ultimate sacrifice on the battlegrounds of Europe.

Masao Sato with fellow members of the 442nd Regimental Combat Team, while on leave in New York City, 1943.

AFTER THE WAR

The war changed Maui forever. After 1945, the island's rigid social foundation reformed in a distinctly different mold. This political and economic makeover did not appear out of the blue, however, but was an outgrowth of long-felt and widespread dissatisfaction.

Although sugar workers had challenged plantation power through walkouts since the turn of the century, none had been truly successful until 1937, when 3,500 Maui members of the Filipino union Vibora Luviminda went on strike for higher wages and won. During the same period, the International Longshoremen's and Warehousemen's Union gained momentum on the premise that all races should unite for the labor cause. One year after the war ended, the labor movement came into its own, when a fractious, violent, but ultimately effective, strike shut down sugar plantations islandwide for 79 days. This landmark action marked a turning point in a campaign to end the age of the paternal plantation and powerless worker. To attain their goal, the labor movement on Maui faced many additional confrontations in the shipping, sugar and pineapple industries over the following decades.

Hand in hand with Hawai'i's shift in labor power came a reversal in politics. Republicans had exercised an iron grip on the electorate for decades. Elections determined which Republican would win, not which candidate. All this was to change almost overnight. Maui's Republican incumbents won handily, as usual, in 1942. Just two years later, island politics turned topsyturvy when Democrats emerged victorious in a plurality of races. Democrats further humbled Republican forces in 1946, when they made a clean sweep of the Board of Supervisors, the equivalent of today's Maui County Council.

The Democrats came to power with the support of the ever-more powerful ILWU. Frustrated by increasing worker demands and emboldened by similar actions across America, management officials accused the ILWU of harboring Communists in its ranks. During a United States House of Representatives hearing by the Committee on Un-American Activities, five Maui labor leaders, along with others from throughout the territory, invoked the Fifth Amendment in their defense. Though cited for contempt of Congress, all were subsequently acquitted.

The ILWU grasp on the Democratic Party eventually lightened, but Democrats continued to dominate local politics with the strong support of newly enfranchised Japanese Americans. Maui's own Patsy Takemoto Mink, a Japanese woman, made remarkable history when she was elected to Congress in 1964.

Another Maui politician, territorial Speaker of the House Elmer F. Cravalho, welcomed a new era when he answered the official call at 10:04 a.m. on March 12, 1959, conveying the news that the Hawai'i Statehood bill had passed Congress. Maui burst forth with joy. Bells pealed, schools dismissed their students, businesses closed and motorcades filled island streets. Bands and marching units led revelers to Maui's most voluble expression of exultation, an extravaganza at the Maui County Fairgrounds. Isle orchestras provided music for celebratory dancing, hula troupes swayed their approval, patriotism overflowed, and each ethnic group, first-class American citizens all, passed in review.

Sugar and pineapple, the driving forces behind Maui's economy for so long, began a slow decline in the 1950s, due to increased labor costs, foreign competition and improvements in alternative sweeteners. The sugar industry responded to these challenges by increasing efficiency through technological innovations, development of by-products, and crop diversification. Hawaiian Commercial & Sugar Company, considered Hawai'i's most efficient plantation, produced 224,000 tons of sugar in 1993, compared to 139,000 tons in 1949. Pioneer Mill also remains viable, although only through worker cutbacks and the cultivation of coffee. Wailuku Sugar Company, on the other hand, is no more. The company, now called Wailuku Agribusiness, has transformed its sugar fields into macadamia orchards and tracts of pineapple, for, despite difficulties, the Maui pineapple industry has survived. The tenacious Maui Land and Pineapple Company maintains the only cannery in the state.

As agriculture weakened, tourism strengthened. The precedent-setting destination resort area at Kā'anapali proved a potent tonic to the struggling visitor industry. The Royal Lahaina Beach Hotel opened in 1962 as the first in a series of planned luxury accommodations and amenities on a strip of Kā'anapali coast almost twice the size of Waikīkī. As tourism fever spread, hotels, condominiums, golf courses, restaurants, and shops spread along the West Maui coast. Further development woke up sleepy Kīhei and fabricated Wailea out of sand and stands of kiawe. In 1951, Maui hosted 14,000 visitors. By 1970, the figure had leaped to over 400,000, with Maui hitting the million mark in 1976. In the 1980s, Maui's visitor count soared along with its reputation. By 1990, over 2,300,000 sunburned and flower-bedecked bodies returned home with precious island memories.

Accompanying Maui's meteoric rise in popularity was a stellar increase in the price one had to pay. A one-bedroom vacation rental with kitchenette in Kīhei in 1970 rented for the daily sum of $12-$18. Today, 75 percent of Maui's 16,800 units exceed $100 a night, with three percent passing the $500 mark. Residents also paid dearly for the island's worldwide acclaim, as high demand for real estate skyrocketed values. For example, a typical home in 1960 sold for $12,000, and in 1970, $32,000. In striking comparison, by 1992, a single family residence cost, on the average, an astronomical $285,000.

Maui experienced a downward slide in population in the 1950s as young people moved to Honolulu or to the mainland for better opportunities. Tourism development not only reversed this population drain, it overcompensated. Tourists who liked what they saw on their island vacation returned as permanent residents, along with former islanders lured home by an improved economy. From a post-war population low of 35,717 in 1960, Maui's headcount had risen to only 38,691 in 1970. In sharp contrast, by 1990 the island was 91,361 strong.

Today Maui struggles to retain the charm of yesteryear. The quality of life that local people value and which attracted so many newcomers is threatened. Efforts to preserve the best of Maui continue, because islanders want to boast with just as much pride in the future as they have in the past, "Maui nō ka 'oi!"

Kahului, with site of current Kahului Airport in foreground, 1923. Note military aircraft parked at airfield on left.

Kahului Airport in the 1960s.

Wailuku, as seen from Kahului, 1940s.

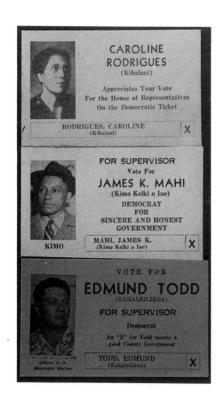

Political advertising cards announcing the candidacy of Democrats for office, late 1940s and 1950s. During this period, the Democrats took over long-Republican Maui politics.

Aerial view of the Maui Mall, shortly after construction. Maui Mall opened in 1971, one year before the Ka'ahumanu Center served its first customers.

An ILWU float parading
down Ka'ahumanu Avenue,
1950s.

Territorial Speaker of the House
Elmer F. Cravalho receiving the
official news that the Hawai'i
Statehood bill has passed Congress,
1959.

Kā'anapali in the 1950s.

Kā'anapali in 1970.

HAWAIIAN RENAISSANCE

It is fitting that someone with the royal blood of a powerful Maui king blazed the trail of Hawaiian self-renewal. Kekaulike descendant John Dominis Holt's seminal work, *On Being Hawaiian*, published in 1974, fanned long smoldering interest in Hawaiian culture, sparking what today is a passion for many, Hawaiians and non-Hawaiians alike. This cultural wildfire has been termed the Hawaiian Renaissance.

Hula, chanting, and crafts have proliferated. Hawaiians study their genealogies, paddle canoes, and pursue traditional agricultural interests. The near-extinct Hawaiian language struggles ever harder to survive, notably at Pūnana Leo o Maui school, where three and four-year-olds use Hawaiian as their first language. These young guardians of the language are now progressing through the Kula Kaiapuni o Maui Hawaiian immersion program at Pāʻia School.

Even more than spectators at Cape Canaveral, Hawaiians thrill at the voyages of the double-hulled canoe Hōkūleʻa, which has logged over 36,000 miles in the last 20 years in its quest to comprehend Polynesian navigation and migrations. Hōkūleʻa stands as both an affirmation of an epic Hawaiian past and an inspiration for the Hawaiian future.

Most of all, Hawaiians want to preserve their beloved ʻāina, their land. The rescue of the island of Kahoʻolawe from its fate as a mili-

tary bombing target focused Hawaiian energy in support of the Protect Kahoʻolawe ʻOhana during the 1970s as it confronted the goliath United States Navy. Citizens of Maui added their special strengths to the organization. PKO member and Keʻanae resident Kimo Mitchell became a martyr to the cause when he and George Helm disappeared at sea during an illegal occupation of the island in 1977. Mauians representative of countless contributors to the PKO vision over the past two decades include Kimo's father, "Uncle" Harry Mitchell, the Kuloloio family, Hōkūlani Holt-Padilla, Burt Sakata, and former Mayor Hannibal Tavares. Ultimately the Protect Kahoʻolawe ʻOhana triumphed. In 1994, the United States Navy returned the island of Kahoʻolawe to the people of Hawaiʻi in a momentous ceremony held on South Maui's Palauea Beach, in sight of the revered isle.

The island of Maui itself has been the site of landmark activism. In 1984, the closing of an 1,100-foot section of the old Mākena road by Seibu Hawaiʻi, developers of the Maui Prince Hotel, hit a Hawaiian nerve. Hawaiians valued the road because it was a section of the ancient Alaloa, or King's Highway, and assured access to the ocean. The Hui Alanui o Mākena, with Dana Nāone Hall as their spokesperson, formed to fight the closing. After a three-year struggle, Seibu agreed to the preservation of the road.

In 1988, the discovery of a vast number of Hawaiian burials at

Honokahua while preparing for the construction of the Ritz Carlton Hotel rallied activists throughout the State. Hawaiians reacted strongly, as they associate a person's mana, or divine power, with their bones. The Hui Alanui o Mākena, along with other groups and individuals, strove to retain the site's sanctity. Negotiations, eased by sensitivity on the part of developer Colin Cameron, resulted in the ultimate relocation of the hotel. The ancient remains of nearly 1,000 Hawaiians ceremonially wrapped in black kapa, were honored with chants and prayers, and replaced in the sacred ground. This highly publicized issue heightened awareness across the islands, prompting a State law establishing local councils dedicated to protecting age-old Hawaiian burials from disturbance.

The 100th anniversary of Queen Liliʻuokalani's overthrow in 1993 attracted more attention to, and support of, the Hawaiian sovereignty movement. Hawaiian sovereignty means different things to different people. Some call for an internationally recognized independent country, while others advocate a self-governing nation within the United States similar to Native American governments on the mainland. And still others favor redress and reparations only. Significantly, President Clinton in 1993 officially recognized the government's wrongdoing by apologizing for the illegal confiscation of the Hawaiian Islands a century ago, but the path to sovereignty remains long and challenging.

Many obstacles litter the route of Hawaiian Renaissance. However, that is to be expected, for most new births go through a demanding labor, not knowing the baby-to-be. What is known is that the child will be a reflection of its parents, the Hawaiian people.

Dana Nāone Hall, Leslie Kuloloio, and members of the Hui Alanui o Mākena, at Honokahua burial site ceremony, 1988.

Leinani Sakamoto and Leʻahi Hall offering hoʻokupu, or gifts, at Honokahua, 1988.

Students at the Pūnana Leo o Maui Hawaiian language preschool, 1990s.

Dancers celebrating the return of Kahoʻolawe to the people of Hawaiʻi, Palauea Beach, 1994.

The opening of the ceremony marking the transfer of Kahoʻolawe from the United States Navy to the State of Hawaiʻi, Palauea Beach, 1994.

Ribbon commemorating the centennial of the overthrow of Queen Liliʻuokalani and the movement toward Hawaiian sovereignty, 1993. ʻOnipaʻa, the motto of the queen, means steadfast.

Mo Moler and Kawaipiʻilani, members of Ka ʻOhana o Kahikinui, on a Hawaiian homestead at Kahikinui, 1993. The inverted Hawaiian flag signifies distress for the Hawaiian nation.

MAUI NŌ KA 'OI - MAUI'S FIRSTS AND FAMOUS

KAMEHAMEHA AND BEFORE

LARGEST AREA OF TARO CULTIVATION IN ANCIENT HAWAI'I - Vast plantings of this staple thrived in an area Hawaiians called Nā Wai 'Ehā from Waikapū to Waihe'e.

Kahului Railroad engine, No. 12, on the day that railroading passed from the Hawaiian scene, 1966.

LARGEST HEIAU IN HAWAI'I - The great Maui chief Pi'ilani dedicated Hāna's Pi'ilani Hale in the 15th century, as a luakini, or war temple.

WETTEST COASTAL REGION IN HAWAI'I - The lush Ko'olau (northeastern) coast from O'opuola Point to Nāhiku supported a dense population of Hawaiians.

ONLY ANCIENT HIGHWAY TO ENCIRCLE A HAWAIIAN ISLAND - Pi'ilani and his son Kihapi'ilani constructed the 138-mile long Alaloa, or King's Highway, in the 16th century. Sections of this engineering feat can still be seen.

FIRST ISLAND CONQUERED BY KAMEHAMEHA I - Even before securing his own home island of Hawai'i, Kamehameha conquered Maui in 1790.

FIRST WESTERN-STYLE HOUSE IN THE KINGDOM - Kamehameha I built a two-story brick "palace" in Lahaina for his beloved Ka'ahumanu in 1802.

RELIGION

FIRST HAWAIIAN BAPTIZED IN THE KINGDOM - Keōpūolani, sacred wife of Kamehameha I, received baptism in Lahaina an hour before her death in 1823, becoming Hawai'i's "first fruit of the mission."

FIRST STONE CHURCH IN THE HAWAIIAN ISLANDS - Lahaina's early missionaries and parishioners constructed Waine'e Church (now called Waiola) in 1828.

FIRST LICENSED HAWAIIAN PREACHER - Pua'aiki, or Bartimeus, the "Blind Preacher of Maui," was licensed at Wailuku in 1841.

FIRST BRANCH OF THE CHURCH OF JESUS CHRIST OF LATTER DAY SAINTS IN HAWAI'I - Elder George Q. Cannon inaugurated Mormonism in Hawai'i at Kealahou in 1851.

EDUCATION

FIRST SCHOOL FOR HAWAIIAN COMMONERS - Missionary and ex-slave Betsey Stockton founded a school for Hawaiians eager for book learning in 1824 at Lahaina.

FIRST HIGH SCHOOL WEST OF THE ROCKIES - Lahainaluna, established in 1831, earned additional distinction as the first boarding school for boys in Hawai'i and the first industrial school of its kind in the United States.

MOST INFLUENTIAL SCHOOL IN THE KINGDOM OF HAWAI'I - Lahainaluna produced Hawai'i's leaders from the 1830s to the 1860s.

FIRST LIBRARY IN HAWAI'I - The Seaman's Chapel and Reading Room, built in Lahaina in 1834, provided for the education and enlightenment of whalers.

FIRST BOARDING SCHOOL FOR GIRLS IN HAWAI'I - Hawaiian girls aged four to ten entered the Wailuku Female Seminary in 1837.

Lahainaluna High School, early 1900s.

Kumu hula Emma Farden Sharpe, a member of the much-honored Farden family.

FIRST HAWAIIAN HISTORICAL SOCIETY - The Royal Hawaiian Historical Society made history themselves in Lahaina in 1839.

FIRST ENGRAVED PAPER MONEY IN HAWAI'I - Printed on heavy squares for use at Lahainaluna in 1843, denominations ranged from three cents to a dollar. Two enterprising students immediately counterfeited the simple notes, making a more elaborate design necessary.

HAWAI'I'S FIRST JUNIOR COLLEGE - Mauna'olu Community College, using the historic Mauna'olu Seminary campus, admitted its first students in 1950.

POLITICS AND GOVERNMENT
FIRST CAPITAL OF THE HAWAIIAN KINGDOM - Lahaina flourished as the seat of royal government from the 1820s until the 1840s.

FIRST HAWAIIAN CONSTITUTION - Hawaiian scholars wrote the constitution of 1840 at Lahaina.

LAND FIRST SOLD TO HAWAIIAN COMMONERS - Nearly 100 parcels in the Makawao district sold to commoners in 1845 in an experiment which led to a system of private land ownership throughout Hawai'i.

FIRST DELEGATE TO CONGRESS FROM THE TERRITORY OF HAWAI'I - Honua'ula-born firebrand Robert Wilcox, elected in 1900 as a member of the Home Rule Party, promoted "Hawai'i for the Hawaiians."

Judge C. Nils Tavares, at right, circa 1922. Tavares was torn between a career as a musician and as an attorney.

THE STATE OF HAWAI'I'S FIRST FEDERAL JUDGE - C. Nils Tavares was appointed to the Federal bench in 1960.

CRIME AND MORALITY
FIRST CODE OF LAWS IN HAWAI'I - In 1824, Ka'ahumanu proclaimed murder, theft, gambling and profaning of the Sabbath to be illegal on the island of Maui.

FIRST TEMPERANCE SOCIETY IN THE ISLANDS - Rampant drunkenness prompted the founding of the Lahaina Temperance Society in 1842.

FIRST BANK ROBBERY IN THE TERRITORY - Within seven days of robbing the Pā'ia branch of the Bank of Hawai'i in 1934, Hawai'i's first holdup men were sentenced by a judge to 20 years at hard labor.

INDUSTRY
THE FIRST GREAT IRRIGATION PROJECT IN HAWAI'I - The Hāmākua Ditch, completed in 1878, paved the way for the rapid expansion of the Hawaiian sugar industry.

FIRST ISLAND TO RECEIVE SCANDINAVIAN IMMIGRANTS - Recruited for work in the sugar fields, Norwegians and Swedes landed at Mā'alaea in the bark *Beta* in February 1881.

FIRST ELECTRICITY IN HAWAI'I - Electric light first radiated in Hawai'i at Spreckelsville Plantation's Mill No. 1 in 1881.

FIRST ISLAND TO RECEIVE PUERTO RICAN IMMIGRANTS - The steamer *Lehua* delivered 56 Puerto Rican sugar workers to Lahaina in December 1900.

BIGGEST SUGAR MILL IN THE WORLD - Hawaiian Commercial & Sugar Company's Pu'unēnē mill, built in 1902, broke world records in sugar production for many years.

FIRST RUBBER INDUSTRY ASSOCIATION IN THE UNITED STATES - Hāna area rubber companies formed the Hawaiian Rubber Growers Association in 1907.

HAWAI'I'S FIRST DESTINATION RESORT AREA - Hawai'i's visitor industry was never the same after the precedent-setting Kā'anapali resort was built in the 1960s.

Haleakalā Highway, shortly after its opening in 1935.

TRANSPORTATION

FIRST LIGHTHOUSE IN HAWAI'I - Erected at Keawaiki in Lahaina in 1840, the first lighthouse stood only nine feet tall.

THE BUSIEST PORT OF CALL DURING MUCH OF THE WHALING ERA - At its peak in 1846, 429 ships anchored in Lahaina Roads.

An early issue of Lahainaluna's **Ka Lama Hawai'i.**

FIRST AND LAST RAILROAD IN THE ISLANDS - Kahului Railroad's locomotive, the *Queen Emma*, inaugurated an auspicious era of Hawaiian railroading when it chugged from Wailuku to Kahului for the first time in 1879, a run that did not end until engine No. 12 screeched to a halt in 1966.

LONGEST AND HIGHEST BRIDGE IN THE TERRITORY - A bridge over Māliko Gulch, completed in 1913, supported Kahului Railroad's extension to East Maui's pineapple fields.

FIRST CAR IN HAWAI'I - Maui sugar planter Henry P. Baldwin's Wood Electric arrived in Honolulu in a shipment of two in 1899.

STEEPEST DRIVE IN THE WORLD - The drive from sea level to the summit of Haleakalā is the greatest elevation gain in the shortest distance in the world.

RECREATION

FIRST BOY SCOUT TROOP IN HAWAI'I - Pā'ia Troop No. 1 pioneered the Hawaiian Boy Scout movement in 1913.

HAWAI'I'S BEST FAIR - The Maui County Fair, begun in 1916, has always been nō ka 'oi, the best!

FIRST ICE RINK IN HAWAI'I - Maui's preeminent county fair show-

Marcelina Santiago, a resident of San Joaquin, Puerto Rico, one of the first 56 Puerto Rican immigrants to Hawai'i.

cased an Ice Follies in 1938. Afterwards, the rink taxed the stamina of a host of weak-ankled island novices.

ART AND MUSIC

FINEST 19TH CENTURY RELIGIOUS ART IN HAWAI'I - These ecclesiastical treasures can be seen at the Holy Ghost Catholic Church in Kula.

OUTSTANDING FAMILY OF HAWAIIAN MUSIC - The Association for Hawaiian Music awarded this honor to the Farden family of Lahaina.

OUTSTANDING WOMAN COMPOSER OF HAWAI'I - Lahaina native Irmgard Farden Aluli has composed hundreds of songs, including "Puamana," "The Boy from Laupāhoehoe," and "E Maliu Mai (Hawaiian Love Call)," since the 1930s.

A TRADITION IN HORSES

FIRST HORSE RIDE IN HAWAI'I - Kamehameha I became the first Hawaiian to ride a horse when three horses were delivered to him in Lahaina in 1803 by Captain Richard J. Cleveland of the HMS *Lelia Byrd*.

MOST RENOWNED HAWAIIAN COWBOY OF ALL TIME - 'Ulupalakua Ranch's head cowboy Ikua Purdy won the World's Steer Roping Championship in 1908.

FIRST HAWAIIAN RODEO CHAMPIONSHIPS - 'Ulupalakua Ranch hosted this paniolo competition in 1939, more than a hundred years after Spanish-Mexican vaqueros arrived to teach Hawaiians the tricks of the cowboy trade.

Robert Wilcox, the territory's first delegate to Congress, as a young man in an Italian military school, 1880s.

FIRST WOMEN'S RODEO IN THE STATE - Maui's hotshot cowgirls have competed in their own rodeo each year since 1974.

HAWAI'I'S BEST RODEO EVENT - All-around honors go to Makawao's annual red, white and blue Fourth of July parade and rodeo.

FLORA AND FAUNA

FIRST MOSQUITOES IN HAWAI'I - Prior to the arrival of the ship *Wellington* at Lahaina in 1826, Hawaiians had never been bothered by the buzz or bite of a mosquito.

FIRST PASSION FRUIT IN HAWAI'I - The flavorful fruit acquired its Hawaiian name from its first home - Liliko'i Gulch, East Maui.

BEST ONIONS - Although farmers grew onions in Kula since the mid-1800s, the mild and flavorful Kula, or Maui, onion first appeared in the early 1930s, courtesy of Kula's vol-canic soil and cool weather in combination with Bermuda onion stock.

COMMUNICATIONS

FIRST NEWSPAPER IN HAWAI'I - The Lahainaluna press printed the first issue of *Ka Lama Hawai'i*, a four-page Hawaiian language weekly, in 1834.

FIRST COMMERCIAL TELE-GRAPH IN HAWAI'I - The message: "God Save the King!" was transmitted via a line stretching five miles from C. H. Dickey's store in Makawao to his home in Ha'ikū in 1877.

FIRST TELEPHONE IN HAWAI'I - In 1878, C. H. Dickey upgraded his telegraphic line and voila! - the first telephone.

FIRST INTER-ISLE TELEPHONE CALL - Conversation flowed across the sea between William Sparks at Kahului Store and John Balch, president of the Honolulu-based Mutual Telephone Company, in 1931.

IN A CATEGORY ALL ITS OWN

STRANGEST CHANGE IN TIME SYSTEMS - Maui changed to Honolulu's system in 1924, thereby gaining 4-1/2 minutes.

HAWAIIAN COWBOYS WIN HONORS AT THE CHEYENNE CONTEST

Purdy Defeats All Comers---Kaaua Takes the Third Place and Jack Low Shows Up Among First Six.

(Cablegram to Hind, Rolph & Co.)

CHEYENNE, Wyoming, August 22.—Purdy, of Hawaii, won the world's steer roping championship at the Frontier Day contest here today. His time was fifty-six seconds. Archie Kaaua took third place and Jack Low sixth.

First, third and sixth places taken by the three representatives from the Hawaiian Islands in the roping contests at Cheyenne yesterday is a record to make every Hawaiian feel proud of the plucky cowboys who traveled across the ocean to the dusty plains of Wyoming to uphold the honor of their native land.

From the brief cablegram above it is shown that Ikua Purdy defeated all

ALOHA, PURDY.

From the sun-dried plains of Texas
From the rolling Northern lands,
From East and West they sent their best,
With chap and spur and flying vest,
And lariats in their hands.

IKUA PURDY—Champion Steer Roper of the world. On his right is ARCHIE KAAUA, who took third place yesterday in the roping contest at Cheyenne

163

MAUI'S MILESTONES

1500s- Kihapi'ilani completes the Alaloa, or King's Highway, begun by his father Pi'ilani.

1736 - Kahekili rules over Maui.

1777 - Ka'ahumanu is born at Ka'uiki, Hāna.

1779 - Captain James Cook sights Maui, but does not land.

1786 - Admiral Jean-Francois de Galaup, Comte de La Perouse, becomes the first Westerner to set foot on Maui.

1790s- Sandalwood trade begins.

1790 - Haleakalā erupts for last time. Kamehameha defeats the forces of Kahekili at battle of Kepaniwai.
Simon Metcalf, captain of the *Eleanora*, kills 100 Hawaiians in Olowalu Massacre.

1795 - Kamehameha conquers Maui for second and final time.

1802 - Kamehameha moves army and fleet to Maui in preparation for attack on Kaua'i.

1819 - North Pacific whaling trade commences.

1820s- Commercial sugar operations begin.

1823 - Reverends William Richards and Charles Stewart, Maui's first Protestant missionaries, arrive in Lahaina.

1824 - Ka'ahumanu creates precedent-setting code of laws.

1825 - Kauikeaouli proclaimed King Kamehameha III at age 12.

1831 - Lahainaluna established.

1834 - Lahainaluna publishes newspaper *Ka Lama Hawai'i*.

1835 - Reverend Jonathan Green founds Wailuku Female Seminary.

1839 - A declaration of rights, known as Hawai'i's Magna Carta, penned by Lahainaluna scholars.

1840 - Lahainaluna scholars compose Hawai'i's first constitution.

1846 - Whaling industry peaks on Maui, 429 ships arrive in Lahaina Roads.
First official Catholic mission

settles at Lahaina.

1849 - California gold boom precipitates rush on Kula potatoes.

1851 - Mormon religion established at Kealahou.

1852 - Chinese imported as labor for sugar plantations.
The *Constitution*, the first steamship to serve the interisland trade, crosses channel between O'ahu and Lahaina.

1854 - Kamehameha III dies after 30 year reign.

1856 - James Makee establishes the Rose Ranch, later known as 'Ulupalakua Ranch.

1860s- Shortage of cotton due to American Civil War causes boom in Mākena.

1861 - East Maui Female Seminary, later called Mauna'olu, founded above Makawao.

1862 - Pioneer Mill Company plants cane in Lahaina.
Wailuku Sugar Company commences business.

1866 - Mark Twain falls in love with Maui.

1869 - Henry Perrine Baldwin goes into historic partnership with Samuel Thomas Alexander in purchase of East Maui land.

1878 - Completion of Hāmākua Ditch allows expansion of sugar industry.
Claus Spreckels acquires 40,000 barren acres of central Maui, establishes Hawaiian Commercial Company, and starts construction of 30-mile ditch system.
Portuguese recruited as plantation laborers.
Charles H. Dickey stretches phone line between his Ha'ikū home and his store in Makawao.

1879 - The Kahului and Wailuku Railroad transports sugar from Wailuku to Kahului Harbor.

1880s- Germans arrive as plantation workers.

1881 - Norwegians and Swedes immigrate.
Electricity comes to Maui.

1886 - Maui Racing Association forms.

1887 - Polo first played.

1888 - Haleakalā Ranch established.

1890s- Scots recruited as plantation managers.

1890 - Dwight D. Baldwin gives birth to isle pineapple industry with plantings in Ha'ikū.

1893 - Queen Lili'uokalani deposed, Provisional Government takes over.

1895 - Officially sanctioned Japanese laborers arrive.

1898 - Alexander & Baldwin purchases Hawaiian Commercial & Sugar Company.

1899 - Italian sugar workers find employment in sugar industry.

1900 - Hawai'i annexed to the United States.
Robert Wilcox elected as territory's first delegate to Congress.
Puerto Ricans land at Lahaina in pursuit of plantation work.
Okinawans supplement sugar industry labor pool.
The Maui News begins publication.
Bubonic plague breaks out in Kahului.

1901 - African Americans join the island labor pool.
Pioneer Hotel (now Inn) established.
Alexander House Settlement begins nearly 50 years of social service.

1902 - Hawaiian Commercial & Sugar Company's Pu'unēnē mill begins operation.

1903 - Koreans add to the island's racial mix.
Ha'ikū Fruit and Packing Company established as pioneer pineapple firm.
Maui Agricultural Company forms from Ha'ikū and Pā'ia

Plantations.

1904 - Wailuku School welcomes students.

1905 - Rubber planted in Nāhiku.
Maui County forms.

1906 - Maui Agricultural Company grinds cane at its new Pā'ia mill.

1907 - Spaniards arrive to work on plantations.
Jack London and wife Charmian first enjoy Maui's pleasures.
Wailuku Courthouse hears first case.

1909 - Russians recruited for plantation labor.
Filipinos begin immigration.

1910 - Kula Sanitorium opens.

1912 - Pineapple planted in West Maui on Honolua Ranch, later to become Baldwin Packers.

1913 - Maui High School opens in Hāmākuapoko.

1916 - The first Maui County Fair entertains fairgoers at Wells Park in Wailuku.

1919 - A disastrous fire destroys much of Lahaina's business district.

1920s - Tandy MacKenzie garners international acclaim as operatic tenor.

1921 - Haleakalā awarded national park status.

1926 - The Belt Road, now called Hāna Highway, links Hāna with the rest of the island.

1927 - Armine von Tempsky publishes her first novel *Hula*.

1928 - 'Īao Theater opens.

1929 - Inter-island air transportation launched.
Dickey-designed Wailuku Library loans first book.

1930 - A massive fire destroys large section of Lower Pā'ia.
Maui's first official airport opens at Mā'alaea.

1932 - Maui Pineapple Company forms from Haleakalā Ranch and Maui Agricultural Company's holdings.

1935 - Mamo Clark stars opposite Clark Gable in *Mutiny on the Bounty*.
Haleakalā Highway dedicated.

1937 - Filipino union Vibora Luviminda strikes for higher wages and wins.

1938 - Kiyoshi Nakama becomes the first of eight national swimming champions to emerge from the coaching of Soichi Sakamoto.
Maui's airport moves to Pu'unēnē.

1940 - Pu'unēnē Naval Air Station built.
Baldwin High School completed.

1941 - Japanese submarines twice attack Kahului.
Maui placed under martial law.

1943 - Kahului Naval Air Station established.

1944 - Camp Maui becomes home to the Fourth Marine Division.
Democrats win majority in isle elections for first time.

1946 - A tsunami severely damages coastal communities, kills 14.
ILWU strike shuts down plantations for 79 days, wins concessions.

1947 - Hotel Hāna Maui welcomes guests.

1948 - Maui Agricultural Company merges with Hawaiian Commercial & Sugar Company.

1950 - The first family moves into Dream City, Kahului.

1951 - The Kahului Shopping Center opens for business.

1956 - First Makawao Rodeo organized.

1959 - Hawai'i becomes State.

1962 - The Royal Lahaina Beach Hotel opens, the first in Kā'anapali.
Hāna Road paved.

1964 - Patsy Takemoto Mink elected to Congress.

1966 - Kahului Railroad ceases operation.

1968 - County inaugurates Mayor Council form of government.
State Building in Wailuku dedicated.

1970 - Development of Wailea begins.

1971 - Maui Mall opens doors to business.

1972 - Maui High School moves to Kahului.
Maui County Building constructed.
Ka'ahumanu Center serves first customers.

1976 - Maui welcomes its one millionth visitor.
Wailea's first hotel, Maui Inter-Continental, welcomes guests.

1977 - Kimo Mitchell and George Helm disappear at sea during illegal occupation of Kaho'olawe.

1978 - Kapalua Bay Hotel registers first guests.

1983 - United Air Lines provides direct service from the mainland to Maui.

1986 - Baldwin Packers pineapple cannery rebuilt as Lahaina Cannery Mall.

1987 - Hui Alanui o Mākena and Seibu Hawai'i agree on preservation of Mākena section of Alaloa.

1988 - Wailuku Agribusiness, formerly Wailuku Sugar, cuts last crop of sugar cane.
Maui County Fair held for last time at historic fairgrounds.
Hawaiian activists rally throughout State for preservation of Honokahua burial site.

1994 - United States Navy turns Kaho'olawe over to the people of Hawai'i in South Maui ceremony.

INDEX

PHOTO CREDITS

Maui Land and Pineapple Company
p.25 Honokahua School; p.31 Charles Keahi; p.34 Emma Sharpe; p.45 Camp 8 Store; p.56 fishermen; p.57 Japanese woman; p.68 pineapple packer; p.71 Honolua ditch; p.72 men loading, Honolua Store; p.73 David Fleming, trimming line, patch, Kahului cannery, 1926; p.75 Honolua Ranch; p.82 Mala Wharf; p.98 football, basketball; p.99 golf course; p.106 fire; p.107 wharf, Honokohau Valley; p.108 hukilau; p.122 Haliimaile, 1930s; p.123 Haliimaile Store; p.152 Jiro Suzawa.

Maui News
p.36 surf article; p.147 cartoon; p.150 shelling Kahului; p.152 Haleakala Dairy.

Masao Sato
p.152 442nd.

Haleakala Ranch
p.63 Benny; p.75 Manduke; p.77 Willie, Haleakala cowboys; p.78 G. Manoa; p.81 Wilder document; p.82 Kahului Railroad document; p.103 H. Amoral, horseracing at Kahului.

Hawaii State Archives
p.12 whale; p.16 Nahienaena; p.27 Malo; p.38 canoe shed; p.56 child; p.105 Front Street, 1940; p.113 Puunene Store; p.130 Enos Store; p.134 fishmarket; p.139 cave shelter; p.163 Hawaiian cowboys.

Nolemana K. Hu
p.61 Sally Orta, Puerto Rican wedding; p.162 first Puerto Rican

Ralph Kagehiro
p.1 Maui the demigod.

Lahaina Restoration Foundation
p.17 map.

Kwan Hi Lim
p.65 Kwan Hi Lim at 14, as actor.

Tom T. Tanizaki,
p.121 Tanizaki family.

William D. Tavares
p.53 H. Tavares; p.54 Territorial legislature; p.161 C. Nils Tavares.

University of Hawaii Manoa, Hamilton Library, Tandy MacKenzie Papers.
p.95 Tandy MacKenzie.

Boogie Wainui
p.37 canoes on beach, B. Wainui and crew.

Private Collections
p.16 Richards; p.20 Pulehu chapel; p.54 processional; p.59 Spanish workers; p.106 Pioneer, 1901; p.108 lumber; p.116 Holy Ghost Church; p.122 Makawao School; p.126 Haiku; p.162 Haleakala Highway.

Carol and Randy von Tempsky
p.75 Louis; p.76 Kaupo; p.89 Jack London; p.95 von Tempsky family, Armine; p.118 Kahikinui; p.119 Kahikinui; p.140 Chu, rest house.

Bren and Fred Bailey Collection
p.3 Hawaiian bowls; p.4 kalo, fisherman; p.5 Kamehameha; p.8 Cook; p.10 fishermen; p.14 Kaahumanu; p.20 Alexander, Ogden, Maigret; p.21 Green, Baldwin; p.24 Lahaina view; p.25 Saint Anthony; p.29 Hawaiian couple, baby, Hawai-

ian girls; p.30 Hawaiian girl; p.33 Maui dancers, hula maidens; p.34 Webber, hula dancers; p.36 surfers, Harry Robello, etc.; p.38 canoes at beach; p.40 Liliuokalani; p.43 Maui workers, Wailuku mill, sugar loading; p.44 Waihee ditch; p.47 hapaha; p.48 Claus Spreckels; p.50 Chinese lady; p.51 Wo Hing Society; p.63 Betsey Stockton; p.71 bango, workers in 1920s; p.73 Hawaiian Pineapple sticker; p.78 milk covers; p.80 SS Haleakala; p.81 ship; p.82 brochure, 1918; p.83 Kahului Railroad card, Kahului Railroad stamps, train; p.85 visitors, 1930s; p.86 postcard; p.87 Inter-Island sticker, boat day postcard, 1922 brochure; p.88 Hawaiian Airlines, hotel sticker, hotel; p.90 O'Keeffe, Mark Twain; p.92 ticket; p.98 Nippon baseball team; p.106 1910 Pioneer, Mala Wharf; p.107 air view - Black Point; p.108 Lahaina (bottom photo); p.110 Paia token, Spreckelsville mill; p.122 parade float; p.125 Maliko Gulch; p.126 Hamakuapoko picnic; p.128 Iao; p.129 Market Street, Saint Anthony; p.130 taxi card, Main Street, Wailuku in 1898; p.133 Kahului waterfront, Kahului in 1940s, Kahului in 1910; p.136 Hana; p.137 ditch trail; p.142 Kihei in 1940s; p.143 Kihei Plantation document; p.148 Fourth Marine; p.154 2 airport photos; p.155 Kaahumanu Avenue, candidates cards; p.156 2 Kaanapali photos, E. Cravalho; p.159 Onipaa ribbon; p.160 Lahainaluna; p.161 Emma Sharpe; p.162 Ka Lama Hawaii; p.163 Robert Wilcox.

Baker-Van Dyke Collection
p.31 Maui grass shack.

Gail Bartholomew
p.93 1916 parade.

Mrs. Frances Cameron Collection
p.123 USO.

Dorothy Chang
p.150 Lahaina storefront.

CynRon Productions
p.117 Keokea town - in memory of Mary K. Yap; p.134 M. Kobayashi Cash Store.

Demetrio Gamponia
p.68 medical card; p.69 policemen, wedding.

Bailey House Museum - Maui Historical Society
p.12 whaling implements; p.19 Bailey House; p.23 Maunaolu; p.24 money; p.44 Hamakuapoko mill; p.50 Chinese funeral; p.51 Eddie Tam, Fong Store; p.59 Molina's Orchestra; p.71 Haiku packing shed; p.107 Pali Road; p.110 Paia Store exterior, Paia Store interior; p.111 Paia town, Paia train station, p.116 Kula Sanitorium; p.129 Market Street in 1890s; p.134 Waikapu; p.137 Hasegawa's; p.148 planes.

Kahului Trucking and Storage
p.48 Maliko; p.85 Kahului Airport; p.133 pier; p.134 flood, railroad wharf; p.156 float; p.160 No. 12.

Ruth Baldwin
p.56 field workers; p.76 Oskie; p.91 fair; p.92 Daisy; p.93 Chu, Royal Hawaiian Band; p.99 tank; p.101 Pukalani stables; p.102 all photos; p.103 Maui team; p.111 truck; p.113 HC&S in 1915, clubhouse in 1915, p.114 Puunene Avenue; p.117 Omaopio; p.119 Ulupalakua, 1928; p.122 church; p.125 Kuiaha depot; p.126 school; p.143 two cattle photos.

Masako Westcott
p.158 2 photos of Hui Alanui o Makena.

M. D. Alborano
p.158 Kahoolawe.

Matthew Thayer
p.159 conch blowing

Ka Ohana o Kahikinui - courtesy of Mo Moler
p.159 Kahikinui.

Bishop Museum
p.3 salt pans; p.4 Lahaina, idol; p.6 spear practice; p.8 La Perouse's ships; p.17 Kauikeaouli; p.40 King Kalakaua, 1879; p.41 Kalakaua in Wailuku, Liliuokalani in Hana; p.47 H. P. Baldwin; p.52 immigrant; p.54 sugar workers in Hana; p.86 bucket; p.137 saloon, Hana in 1883; p.139 wedding; p.142 Kihei Wharf; p.143 Koa House; p.145 school; p.148 beach.

Alexander & Baldwin Corporation
p.57 Jodo Band; p.92 fairground; p.97 sumo; p.99 Coach Sakamoto; p.111 Harry Baldwin; p.114 camp; p.155 Maui Mall.

Toshio Ansai Family
p.57 Toshio Ansai.

Napoleon Agasid
p.150 war bonds.

Karen Anna
p.122 Makawao.

Hawaii Chinese History Center, Honolulu
p.51 Sun Yat Sen.

DeSoto Brown Collection
p.90 Frank Sinatra; p.95 Mamo Clark, 1935 and 1937.

Maui Public Library
p.123 bookmobile.

Memory Lane Antiques
p.92 County Fair sheet music.

Henry E. Meyer, Jr.
p.59 Hyman J. Meyer, J. Johansen.

Ruth Kihm Molina
p.65 Korean woman; p.66 Christian church, Korean woman.

Olivia Pacheco
p.150 gas mask.

Winona Paschoal
p.134 Iao Theater

Puerto Rican Heritage Society - Boricua Hawaiian Collection
p.60 troubador.

Punana Leo Maui Hawaiian Language School
p. 158 school children.

Men of Hawaii, 1930.
p. 62 Crockett.

In Freedom's Cause, 1947.
p.151 three servicemen.

Notices of the Life, Character and Labors of the Late Bartimeus Puaaiki of Wailuku, Maui Hawaii, 1844.
p.27 Bartimeus.

Alan Haili
p. 30 Sam Kalama